Avoiding 1984

Books by Robert Theobald published by Swallow Press.

An Alternative Future for America II: Essays and Speeches,
1970, rev. ed.
Middle Class Support: A Route to Socioeconomic Security,
1972
Economizing Abundance: A Non-inflationary Future, 1970
Teg's 1994: An Anticipation of the Near Future, with J. M.
Scott, 1972
An Alternative Future for America's Third Century, 1976
Avoiding 1984: Moving Toward Interdependence, 1982

Avoiding **1984**

Moving Toward Interdependence

Robert Theobald

Swallow Press — Ohio University Press
Chicago   Athens, Ohio   London

TO

those who will act to avoid
the potential disasters of the eighties
and to create a more human society

Swallow Press Books
are published by
Ohio University Press
Athens, Ohio 45701

Library of Congress Cataloging in Publication Data

Theobald, Robert.
  Avoiding 1984.

  1. United States—Social conditions—1945–
2. Social prediction. 3. Social change.
4. International cooperation. I. Title.
HN65•T4424   303•4'973   82–6501
ISBN 0–8040–0400–5   AACR2
ISBN 0–8040–0429–3 (pbk.)

Contents

CONTENTS

Introduction

1984.

The year of the next presidential election and quite probably the year of the next British election.

The year in which George Orwell placed his classic anti-utopian book, *1984,* which describes a nightmare world of scarcity, wanton cruelty, fascism, and constant warfare.

George Orwell's imaginary universe and our real world will not be identical. However, unless we mobilize additional willpower and wisdom we shall see a continuation and worsening of the immediate threats already posed by excessive levels of personal stress and consequent violence. We shall watch the possibilities for individual self-development decline. George Orwell will be essentially right. Indeed, the potential for a world holocaust, similar to Neville Shute's prophecies about eventual *all-out* nuclear warfare in *On the Beach,* is still growing.

The dangers which confront us can be effectively overcome. We know enough to change directions for the better. There are few people, however, who are ready to use their knowledge to inform vigorous action. This situation will not alter significantly until individuals are convinced of the certainty of disaster if we continue on our present course and are equally convinced of the possibility for improving mankind's conditions if we should act creatively.

The Chinese have long been aware of this twofold necessity. Their symbol for the word *crisis* contains two characters: one for danger and one for opportunity. The danger comes if profound changes in conditions are ignored and social practices are continued after they have become inappropriate. The opportunity emerges if the profound changes are understood and new solutions are created so that they can be adopted when the crisis *is perceived* as acute by those with the ability to make decisions.

The word *perception* is critical here. Decisions are governed by perceptions of reality. The small-scale and the peripheral are often blown up and get all the attention while the long-run, fundamental changes are often ignored. True crises therefore often result in a worsening of conditions because the necessary new thinking has not been done.

This is an inevitable human pattern. We are all naturally committed to maintaining the patterns by which we structure today's complex realities. Fundamental alterations in perceptions are stressful and unsettling. They necessarily affect the way in which we think and act, leading John Maynard Keynes to observe that in the long run it is even more stressful and dangerous to deny the reality of change when it is, in fact, taking place.

If we continue to fail to change our perceptions—to move beyond despair and to accept fundamentally new understandings— then world breakdown is inevitable. There is a disturbing cautionary tale about frogs placed in a saucepan of cold water. If the temperature is raised with sufficient slowness the frogs will stay in the water until they boil to death.

For the last twenty years, the global temperature has been rising. We shall either choose to jump out of the water soon or our energy will be so vitiated by the heat that we shall be unable to move at all. It is in this context that we should be grateful to the Republicans, whose policies are clearly based on the belief that there have been no profound changes in the last three decades and that the models of the fifties can still be effective if only they are carried through with energy and imagination. The attempt to turn back the clock to the fifties will inevitably fail. As crises develop, societies will have a chance to "perceive" the traps in which we are caught. But effective decision making will only occur if enough of us work toward this goal and imagine profoundly new directions which recognize the many profound revolutions of the present time. Three of the most crucial are the weaponry revolution, the cybernetic revolution, and the human rights revolution. These were set out as early as 1964 in a report entitled "The Triple Revolution," of which my wife and I were authors with others. The report was sent to President Johnson and was widely printed and quoted. The central arguments were that:

—the weaponry revolution has made warfare an impossible means of settling disputes. Suggestions that the nuclear genie can be stuffed back into the bottle are irrelevant while the idea that warfare between the great powers will not involve nuclear weaponry is naive and irresponsible. Disputes must therefore increasingly be settled by negotiation, mediation, and arbitration if the destruction of the human race is to be avoided.

—the cybernetic revolution, which links computers and machines, will remove the need to use brains in production just as the industrial revolution freed up men's muscles. The Neo-Keynesian commitment to provide jobs for all who want them is therefore neither feasible nor desirable.

—the human rights revolution is leading people to demand more opportunities for self-development. On the one hand, this can lead to self-indulgence and a "me-generation." On the other, it can provide the potential to develop the more intelligent and creative people needed to manage the world we are creating for ourselves.

Politicians in the early eighties are trying to stop irreversible tides of technological, economic, and social change. They are acting directly against the real revolutions of today. The United States, in particular, is committing itself to being the "strongest" power in the world: this concept is meaningless in the nuclear era and can only ensure mutual destruction. In addition, the acceptance of this goal will move scarce human resources away from urgent social and economic needs, will cause deep cuts in social services, and will increase inflation.

The United States is also committing itself to maximum economic growth and maximum rates of increase in productivity. This will lead to the rapid installation of computers and robots and the displacement of human beings who will not be able to find alternative jobs, thus enhancing frustration and unrest.

Finally, the United States has largely rejected the Carter administration's commitment to human rights. This commitment was naive at times and was often badly handled. It recognized, however, the need for world standards led and supported by the rich nations of the world. Abandonment of such a human rights stand increases dramatically the dangers of international terrorism.

How long will it be before we recognize that we cannot turn back the clock? It is impossible to know. But in a profound sense the question is irrelevant because we shall require every possible moment if we are to develop a new understanding which will support the needed creative responses that move beyond the current sterile debate between the left and the right.

The human race will either grow up or blow itself up. These stark options must be faced. We must cease to bury them beneath meaningless verbiage which promises what cannot be delivered.

* * *

This book is based on the belief that most people in America and throughout the world are today surprised, shocked, and confused by the developments which are taking place around them. They perceive the need for change, but they do not yet know what to do about it. As a result, they are not ready to make the critical decisions which are so urgently required.

The breakdown we face today emerges from the institutional denial of the reality of change. Polls have repeatedly shown that individuals are personally aware of the need to recognize new realities. But the rhetoric of politicians and bureaucrats, of intellectuals and the media remains essentially unaltered. People feel that they are going mad because their perception of the world—as compared to the conventional wisdom—is so different. One of the most common reactions to my speeches is: "Thank you for showing that I'm not crazy."

We have lived for almost a decade within a "conspiracy of silence." The best informed people have been increasingly aware of the necessity for fundamental change. But most of them have not been prepared to puncture the complacency into which the rich countries have sunk. Only as the depths of the eighties' dangers are becoming clear is a recognition dawning that not only does the "emperor have no clothes on" but that it is up to us as citizens to find him coverings before he freezes to death. His courtiers appear unable to perceive uncomfortable realities: even if they do, they are apparently unwilling to break through the limitations of court etiquette!

We can only be effective in clothing the emperor if we recognize the immense amount of effort which is needed to break out of the stereotypes and traps into which we have all individually and collectively fallen. Thus, this book will not provide slick, final answers to the problems we presently perceive. Indeed, its goals are the opposite. We shall learn that we shall be constantly surprised in the future and that unexpected events will almost certainly require fundamental changes in direction, some of which have hardly been considered up to the present time.

All of us need to examine new ideas which will often disrupt current hopes and beliefs. The first "natural" reaction to such material may well be rejection and anger. Killing the messenger who brings bad news is a long-ingrained tradition, but we can no longer afford to continue it. We must gain a better sense of the *broad range* of alternative futures which lie ahead of us so as to prevent the secondary and tertiary results of our activities from warping or even negating our original intentions.

It is now generally accepted that the future we inherit comes into existence because of our hopes and fears and the actions we take as a result of our perceptions. Our personal futures, and those of our society as a whole, are largely created as self-fulfilling and self-denying prophecies.

In one sense we are learning that we should enlarge the scope of a traditional saying to young people: "Be very careful what you want, you may get it." Today we need to recognize as a *society* that "we must all be careful what we want for we may *indeed* get it." Do we really want what we say we want, and if we do, is what we want feasible? Further, is what we want as a society and as individuals compatible?

Even these questions do not push us far enough. Today, the views of various groups are so contradictory that no effective decision-making is possible. Each group, in addition, is so certain of the disastrous consequences which will follow if their particular approaches are not accepted that they are prepared to disrupt decision-making processes at all levels in order to make sure that their views prevail.

We have no shared vision about what is feasible and desirable. We are rapidly losing our belief that it makes sense to work with others to discover the root causes of our disagreements. We face the situation described by W. B. Yeats:

Things fall apart, the center cannot hold, Mere anarchy is loosed upon the world.

This book then is a way of "contexting" reality. Most citizens today are thoroughly confused by the endless, repetitive, contradictory streams of information which reach them about contemporary issues. More and more people are giving up the attempt to understand the world in which they live, seeing this task as impossible. The material here tries to illuminate the agreements and the disagreements which exist among those who try to think about the future and its prospects.

One further point needs to be made. Most sets of policy proposals, as well as future-oriented computer games and simulations, state what should be done but efficiently hide the assumptions, complexities, and compromises inherent in the proposals. This material, on the contrary, aims to clarify the overall picture and to enable the *eventual* resolution of disagreements.

To avoid disappointment, you should know what this book will not do. It contains no rules of thumb, no magic panaceas which will lessen the need for intelligent decision-making. On the other hand, the ideas contained in this book should enable individuals and groups to focus more effectively on the ways in which priorities for both thought and action can be established.

This book will only be useful if it leads to new ideas and to an increase in creativity. It is therefore based on a set of ideas about how people learn, which are set out with extreme brevity here.

Effective learning always requires an understanding of the context. Place most Americans in the middle of Tibet in the winter and they may well die rather than cope. Place Tibetans in Manhattan and the result is likely to be equally disastrous. One can only learn if one has the understanding which can be tied to new patterns of thought and action.

The ideal climate for fundamental learning develops when bright, intelligent people are brought together with each other in a well-designed "psychic space" which encourages new thinking and breaks through the barriers to communication. This ideal climate is difficult to achieve in many cases, and learning aids, like the material presented in this book, can provide people with ideas which may start the flow of creativity. But, these aids or guides should be abandoned whenever they stop helping and start hindering the creative juices.

Such open communication processes can stimulate new thinking for individuals and the group as a whole. These processes can eventually lead to ideas which are either unusual or even "new" within the culture and cause individuals and institutions to change their patterns of decision-making.

Creativity, however, is not a tidy pattern and one does not invent to order. Ideas which emerge from open processes will often force new directions on the individual and the organization, for it will become clear that the meeting of fundamental societal goals requires new means. Thus there will always be resistance to opportunities for creativity by those who are so immersed in day-to-day crises that any new input will overload them and make them less efficient.

ORGANIZATION OF THE BOOK

This material depends on an understanding of how different reality seems at different periods of time. Thus, the first section of this book sets out the life patterns of fictional characters who lived in the twentieth century. The different directions and life priorities will, it is hoped, provide a sense of the extraordinary changes which have taken place—and will take place—in a single century.

The second section then sets out several scenarios for the directions in which America may move in the next two decades. It should be stressed that these are not prophecies which are expected to come true in detail. Rather they are ways of helping you to think through what might happen. They are designed to challenge your thinking, not present inevitabilities. Each of the scenarios is, of course, radically oversimplified. To get a full sense of what might happen in any possible future requires, at the very least, a full-length book.

The third section is a series of brief reports from a task force to the key foundations in the country which are considering whether it is possible to draw the scope of change to the attention of American citizens. Each of these reports takes up one driving force which will continue to affect events strongly throughout the rest of the century regardless of what may be done by policy makers.

The fourth section is designed to show how social policies may vary depending on the directions and emphases which develop in coming years. The pressures on the natural resource base, for example, are going to be very different in a society which opts for a high-growth and high-technology future as compared to issues which will emerge if we opt for far lower rates of growth in a decentralized society.

Similarly, the American economy will evolve very differently in various possible futures. We have become so used to our commitment to full employment that we no longer examine the costs of this commitment or its feasibility in the long run. This commitment may, in fact, have to be reconsidered in the immediate future.

The fifth section will consider the implications of the future we must create for education and management. It will also suggest that *you* can and should be involved.

* * *

Am I fooling myself in writing this book? Is the real future affected by our actions? Or are we actually pawns of forces too big for us to affect, or perhaps even comprehend?

The power and influence of human beings over events is one of the classical philosophical questions: some believe that there is no control over events while others believe we can act as we wish. I shall state but not argue my own position here: there are times, of which this is one, when the direction of events depends directly on the patterns of action of individuals and groups because the balance is somewhat equally poised and can move in several directions depending on intelligence, creativity, and sheer guts.

Indeed, this book itself illustrates this thesis in a limited way. I was asked to speak to the United States Department of Agriculture in 1979 on the future of renewable natural resources. I stated that the problem in the United States was that we really only considered one possible future with some minimal variations around it. I went on to argue that we would be forced to choose, in the near future, either through conscious decision or default, between mutually incompatible directions. I argued further that management of our future would be impossible until we recognized this reality. To drive home my point, I entitled my speech: "Why Effective Decision Making is Currently Impossible."

This harsh approach represents my normal style. I bring my audiences what I think they *ought* to hear rather than what they would be comfortable with. Normally the result is that I am thanked politely—or not so politely—but it is made abundantly clear that I shall not be invited to return. The pattern with USDA was different —they commissioned a manual which would help their staff perceive the varying directions for the future and to choose between them.

This experience, and others like it, have proved to me over and over again that condemning bureaucrats for inflexibility and lack of imagination is as stupid and irresponsible as deriding men or women, or old people or young people, or those in power or those out of power, *as a group.* Our need is to form a coalition of *all* those who are prepared to rethink and be pro-active at this critical time.

Some of the material reproduced here comes, after revision, from the manual, which has already helped in small but significant ways to change the styles and directions of thinking within USDA and has influenced other federal bureaucracies. A further development from this work was the creation of a computer-based learning system on the future in general, and particularly on the future of renewable natural resources.

I want therefore to thank John Okay of the Soil Conservation Service of USDA and also Bob Bergland, the then secretary of agriculture, who was highly supportive. I acknowledge with thanks the efforts of various top-level bureaucrats who successfully broke through the inevitable barriers to new ideas. I must also express my deep gratitude to Peter and Trudy Johnson-Lenz who worked closely with me throughout this project and were the chief architects of the computer-based learning system based on the manual.

Finally, I must mention the style used in the body of this book. You are provided with a comments column in which you can write your reactions, ideas, and thoughts. This is an interactive book to which you need to respond as much as you need to read, for without your active involvement there is no real chance that your action patterns will alter. At the end of the book, you are offered wide opportunities for further involvement in this type of thinking and action if you should be interested.

1 Twentieth-Century Life Histories

The process of birth, maturation, and death has not changed fundamentally in all human history.

However, the ways in which we see the world and the opportunities we can grasp have altered dramatically even over the last century. The fictional biographies which follow provide a sense, it is hoped, of the differences which have developed and the further changes which are possible in this century.

I hope that some of you will take the time to write up other patterns which did exist or may come to exist. I have ended my biographies in the year 2001. You may want to be more adventurous and write forward to the year 2051.

Joan 1911–

Joan was born in Britain in 1911 to lower-middle-class parents. She was one of four children. Her father was killed at the Somme during the First World War.

Joan's mother was attractive, and she remarried a teacher in 1921. He was a remarkable man, far ahead of his time in his attitudes, who cared as much for his stepdaughters as for his stepsons. There were two further children born during the second marriage. One of the stepdaughters died of pneumonia in 1932.

The twenties were a good period. Incomes, while still low, were rising, and they were quite adequate to raise a family of six within the standards of the time. In 1929, just before the slump, Joan won a scholarship to Cambridge—a remarkable event for the time.

She decided to study economics and learned her theory during the Great Depression. She gained a "first"—the highest honor she could receive—and immediately gained entry to the British civil service. Acceptance here confirmed her talent.

Joan was an early convert to Keynesian ideas, studying with Keynes himself, and struggled to see these ideas introduced more widely during the second half of the thirties. As soon as the worst days of the war were over, Joan was delighted to be nominated to the team which planned for the end of the war. She was able, with others, to ensure the acceptance of Keynes's ideas. Unfortunately, however, the team underestimated the level of pent-up demand that would exist at the end of the war, and this miscalculation made it more difficult for Britain to readjust.

queries
and
comments

By 1955, when Britain seemed well on its way to recovery, Joan felt that she wanted new challenges. She joined the economics division of the United Nations and two years after her arrival married a French translator, Edouard, who was working at the Chase Manhattan Bank. They met originally at the première of a new ballet.

Joan found herself frustrated by the blindness of the United Nations toward the magnitude of the development problem. Moving beyond Keynes, she saw that new theory was required as well as a clear concept that development was a cultural as well as an economic question. The documents prepared for the first development decade in 1960 were a deep disappointment to her.

She stayed on with the United Nations until 1965, but she felt that she was achieving nothing. She went back to the British civil service after ten years and found that morale and quality of service had fallen off significantly compared to her previous experience. Edouard, like all translators, found no difficulty in obtaining work in Britain. The last years of Joan's working life were spent worrying as she saw the consequences of the spread of self-centered decision making.

Joan retired early and went back with Edouard to France: this had been their agreement when they left the United Nations. They lived in Nimes in the south of France, where Edouard's ancestors had been born. The troubles of the eighties passed them by, to a large extent, because Joan's government pension and the couple's investments in land held up well compared to those of many others. Like everybody else, their standard of living is lower in the year 2001 than it was in the middle of the twentieth century, but then they don't expect anything else.

Joan is a remarkable ninety-year-old. She feels that she has had a good life. She watched the worldwide celebration of the summer solstice and commented: "I would never have believed that we could have achieved so much in one century. Yes, we made mistakes as economists but we were also part of the process which has led to this extraordinary moment. I'm proud to be a part of the human race."

Bill 1931–2001

Bill was born in 1931 to an American middle-class family; he had an older sister. He was almost entirely sheltered from the effects of the Depression because his father retained his job throughout the period.

Bill was also sheltered from the Second World War. His father was not liable for military duty. Despite some limited rationing, the

effect of the conflict on him was minimal, and he has never understood why people born in Europe at the same time were so scarred
by the experience, even if they did not get near the fronts.

Bill's introduction to reality came when he served in Korea.
He was invalided home following a leg wound which left him with
a slight limp. Following his return, he went to Harvard where his
family had sent its children for three successive generations. He met
a Radcliffe girl, married her and had three children.

Bill had been bitten by the computer bug by the time he
completed his Harvard work. He believed that the huge clumsy
systems would eventually be reduced in size and cost to the point
where they would have a dominant influence on the direction of
world society.

In 1954, therefore, he went on to postgraduate work at the
Massachussetts Institute of Technology. He was recruited by IBM
and was one of the most important members of various critical
development teams.

By 1963, Bill was recognizing that the computer would have
far greater impacts on society than most people in the company and
elsewhere were willing to understand. He read and was fascinated
by "The Triple Revolution" which placed great weight on the implications of computers and robots, as well as on the drive for human
rights and the consequences of ever more destructive weaponry.

Bill approached his bosses about this subject and initially was
asked to help develop an internal position on the subjects and issues
he had raised. But as his ideas developed, he found that he was
threatening his peers. While he was getting support from some
members of top management, this support was being diluted—and
even reversed—by middle management.

Confronted by this situation, Bill recognized that he either had
to forget about his concerns or leave the company. He chose the
latter course in 1969 and developed his own consulting organization
which came to concentrate on the ways in which the new technologies could benefit firms, other organizations, and the total society.
His wife divorced him in the early seventies. Fortunately, the children were grown, but Bill found the stress very great indeed.

Building up a roster of clients was not easy because Bill's
insistence on looking at the broad issues seemed wasteful and costly
to many companies and government agencies. But Bill was highly
competent, and his insistence on looking at the broader issues paid
off in better consumer and worker relations and often even in higher
profits.

By 1980, when Bill was forty-nine, he was in an extraordinary
position to take advantage of the growing demand for help in coping

3

with the implications of the microelectronic revolution. He made many hard decisions at this point: one was to continue to work for himself rather than to create a firm. He cooperated with other self-actualizing people on specific projects as this appeared appropriate.

Bill stayed at the forefront of the Electronic Information Exchange System designed at the New Jersey Institute of Technology, originally with federal support and later on a commercial basis. Indeed, he first met his second wife, Doreen, through interaction on the system. They became an increasingly close-knit team in the second half of the eighties.

By 1988, Bill felt in need of fundamental renewal. Taking advantage of one of the support processes which had been created during the decade, he and his wife lived on the big island of Hawaii and developed a new variety of hibiscus.

They then came back and both of them made significant life-cycle changes. Bill spent the nineties developing a world language based on fundamentally new understandings of communications. His wife, on the other hand, moved into the arts as a conscious myth-maker.

By the summer solstice of the year 2001, Bill and Doreen were both very sick. They decided, after very careful consideration and discussion with their children, their friends and their colleagues, to use the suicide center which was now available for those who felt that they were subtracting from their lifetime achievements rather than adding to them by continuing to exist.

Sammy 1951–

Sammy was born in 1951 in the highlands of Scotland. His first decade fell in an expansionary period of history, but the seventies saw the continuing tightening of the financial vise in the United Kingdom.

Sammy was bright enough to overcome all the hurdles to gaining a university place and studied biology and bio-ethics at Edinburgh University. However, due to the university cuts of the early eighties, his postgraduate work had to be done in Canada, where he met his wife Samantha. But even in Canada the situation was very difficult in the eighties, and finding a satisfactory job took great time, effort, and, above all, perseverance. Nevertheless, eventually Sammy did get work with a citizens' group whose primary goal was the development of a problem/possibility focuser on bio-ethics.

Sammy stayed in touch with Scotland. Indeed, like so many people who had been born there, he looked increasingly for ways to get home again. He watched with wonder as the Scottish intellectual tradition was renewed and was delighted to receive an offer to teach at the Highland University located in Dingwall and funded by those private interests which saw and accepted their responsibility for better educational facilities. This was part of the movement away from central government activities.

Sammy originally felt that he could not accept this job because of his commitment to Samantha. He was amazed when a job was also offered to her and thus learned that the industrial-era bias against husband and wife teams was progressively decaying in Scotland.

The biological revolution developed almost more rapidly than Sammy had hoped—and in some senses—feared. By 1990, many of the central dilemmas of the society were resulting from it. We were learning by this time that we should strive to bring healthy children into the world and that the creation of "life" was not a sufficient goal.

Struggles were also beginning about the implications of the phrase "the improvement of the human race." What did we mean by this term? Was this a viable goal for which to strive? Could we anticipate what skills and talents and genes the human race would require in future generations?

Meanwhile, Samantha was helping to use the new biological knowledge to cope with the food crisis. Conventional agriculture had proved incapable of raising food production enough to take care of the growth of population. But a number of new techniques had been devised to show the potential for growing food more rapidly.

By 1995 both Samantha and Sammy were exhausted. They decided to enter the community at Iona in Scotland as "aunt" and "uncle" and to spend a period of years there gaining the human experience they felt they had missed as a result of their concentration on their intellectual work.

2001 led to a further change for them. They said farewell to their community and left, on one of the modern sailing boats, for South Africa to lend their skills to recreate community after the disastrous struggles of the late eighties and nineties.

Teg 1973–

Teg was born in 1973 in Arizona. The struggles of the seventies and eighties caused her family to move to Quebec where she lived in one of the domed cities which proved to be energy savers in the North.

Teg was in the first generation that went back to the creative and conscious use of rites of passage, helping people to move from one period of their life to another. Certain families and communities had discovered by this time that people do need to have these transitions dramatized.

She was lucky in her teachers: one of them, in particular, enabled her to grasp world dynamics and inspired in her a concern for social entrepreneurship. Her ideas were so interesting that she was awarded an Orwell fellowship in 1994. The Orwell Foundation was created in 1984 as a "thank-you" to George Orwell whose dramatization of the dangers of this period allowed the worst dangers to be avoided.

Teg used her Orwell fellowship to travel around the world. Teg made her fair share of mistakes, as is inevitable at her age, but she was able to perceive that the concentration of communities upon their own needs was fragmenting the necessary global understandings.

Her insights were seen as so important that they were widely circulated under the title *Teg's 1994*. Teg herself was invited to join the Terran Communication Council in Hawaii, an organization created in the 1980s to enable communication and joint decision making among those most competent to understand world dynamics. Its members were chosen in terms of their capabilities: those who were asked to serve often saw the honor as one they would have preferred to avoid, but refusal was unthinkable.

Teg played an active part in the creation of the worldwide coalition which led to the 2001 summer solstice activities. She chose to leave the Terran Communication Council at this time and is now planning to spend the next ten to fifteen years raising a family of one boy and a girl.

Her marriage to George was formalized during the summer solstice. George was an old friend from Quebec who had been busy learning about the contexts in which psychic phenomena could be effective.

Jim 1991–

Jim was born in 1991 in Wales. By the age of ten he had a range of experiences using the talents available in the community and the electronic media which would have been exceptional for a twenty-one-year-old even one generation ago.

The concept of lockstep schooling has been abolished in Jim's community. He benefited from the results of a battery of computer-based physiological and psychological tests starting from the time he was born. These were used to determine aptitudes and to start the process of development to ensure the actualization of Jim's personal skill pattern. Those most competent in the areas which interested Jim were then asked to develop a curriculum which would be most effective given the greatly increased knowledge of patterns of child development.

By the age of seven, after the first rite of passage, Jim was expected to take considerable responsibility for his own individual schooling. As is quite typical, a great deal of the rite of passage was taken up with explaining to him what was known about his strengths and weaknesses so that he could participate in future decisions about his life course.

The primary shift between Jim's socialization patterns and those of earlier generations is that Jim is expected to understand his mind, his body, and his spirit. The good life, Jim's community believes, must be the examined life.

Jim's age group took upon themselves the creation of an extraordinarily moving myth of death and rebirth at the time of the summer solstice celebrations. It was the highpoint of the local event for many. The ability of all those involved to use Welsh as a matter of course was a source of great joy to those who feared that the language might have died out by the end of the century.

queries
and
comments

2 Alternative Scenarios: Year 2000

All of us have implicit beliefs about the future. But, we often find it difficult to state these beliefs in open and creative ways so that others can help us reconsider how valid our patterns of thinking really are.

The material which follows is designed to help you imagine yourselves forward into the year 2000 and to contrast different visions of the directions in which people expect the world to move over the next twenty years. You will find four contrasting views here: a status quo scenario; a high–technology, high–growth scenario; a low–technology, low–growth scenario; and a management/transformational scenario.

You may well find it difficult to imagine yourself forward into the year 2000. So let us start with an easier exercise, which may be aided by the life scenarios you have already read.

Imagine yourselves *backward* to the year 1963. How much culture shock would you experience if you were suddenly back in the early sixties? How would your present attitudes mesh with those which you would discover among people living at that time? Would you be generally uncomfortable or very comfortable? What values, styles, and attitudes of this earlier period would you find most attractive, which most destructive, which most hypocritical, which most "surprising?" Were you alive in 1963?

Before you start to imagine the future, take time to think seriously about "time travel" into the past. You need to recognize the amount of change which *has* taken place if you are to face up to the speed of change in the future.

Once you have done this, you will feel, it is hoped, more ready to deal with future changes. The four scenarios you will study in this section are all dated in the year 2000. One way of looking at the material is as a number of different documents which could be written by coexisting groups. This might seem at first sight absurd: however, if you read today's publications, it is clear that people and groups observe the "same reality" and come up with totally different perceptions of what is actually going on, let alone what should be done to improve the directions of the culture. Another way to look at the four scenarios is to consider them as the outside limits of the probable. They can be seen as containing many of the elements which could eventually be meshed into a more desirable future for the United States. Finally, of course, one can treat each document as a different "future history."

Before describing the various scenarios it is essential to mention one *set* of scenarios which has been excluded from this material. There is a significant number of people who argue that a collapse of the world socioeconomy is already inevitable because we shall be unable to deal with the issues which presently confront us. Those advancing these views produce a broad range of arguments which quite often seem compelling. The reason that collapse scenarios are not included here is that this book is designed to help us do better in the future than in the past. It is, therefore, a waste of time to examine those patterns which would make it impossible for the society to function at all. This does not mean that collapse is impossible: it means that *we* must prevent it.

The four scenarios included are:

1. *STATUS QUO SCENARIO*   This is the president's State of the Union message for the year 2000. After severe problems in the eighties, the world has come back, and slow and steady progress is once again being made. The major problem is that levels of tension are still rising between the rich and the poor countries of the world and that no way out of this situation has yet been perceived.
2. *HIGH–TECHNOLOGY, HIGH–GROWTH SCENARIO* This is a *Wall Street Journal* lead article of January 1, 2000, delivered to the subscriber's house by facsimile production. Once the United States regained its nerve, it proved possible to overcome the transient difficulties of the seventies and to increase the standard of living at a rate never achieved in the past.
3. *LOW–TECHNOLOGY, LOW–GROWTH SCENARIO* This is posted on a wall in a commune. The situation in the United States was turned around during the eighties so that the primary social drive became a desire for a more effective pattern of living within environmental limitations.
4. *MANAGEMENT/TRANSFORMATIONAL SCENARIO* This report comes from the Terran Communication Council. It emphasizes the progress that has been made in developing skills to achieve better management. This scenario is heavily reliant on high levels of telecommunications and uses "appropriate" technology to achieve those goals which are seen to be desirable by the society.

queries
and
comments

9

As you work with these scenarios you may first want to criticize those parts that do not appear coherent with the other ideas in the same scenario. You may want to discuss your criticisms with others. As you become more confident, you may want to write your own scenario—either as a variant of one of those in this guide or in a completely new way.

In addition, you may want to compare the feasibility of the various scenarios. What would have to happen to make each scenario work? Does each scenario convince you that its parts hang together? Which scenario do you believe is the most feasible and the most desirable? And finally, how would you act *personally* to ensure its creation?

In the next part of this book, additional information about the various driving forces in the society will be introduced. This will challenge some of the conventional wisdom. As you read this section of the book, you may find your assumptions about possible and desirable scenarios shifting. But the first step is to find out what you currently believe.

Transcript of the State of the Union Message in the Year 2000

My Fellow Americans,

I am delighted to give the State of the Union message for the year 2000 and to inform you of the directions in which I believe that we can and should move in the years to come.

As you are well aware, I am only the second president to serve a nonrenewable six–year term as the result of the 30th Amendment to the Constitution. My predecessor established a tradition which I believe to be valid and I shall continue. He set out the critical issues which he thought the next election debate should cover. Despite the fact that he was not of the same party, I am delighted to acknowledge that his lack of personal self–interest gave him a degree of credibility and effectiveness in his last year in office which was certainly not expected by the opponents of the six–year–term amendment.

My goal today will therefore be to draw a fair balance sheet of the state of the union at this time. I am only too well aware that my position necessarily determines my perceptions, and I have therefore asked two groups outside the government to provide very brief statements of their views and have included them as an integral part of my speech.

As always, we are confronted with very different views of the future. There are several groups which remain convinced that we

queries
and
comments

could move into a bright new era if only their ideas were fully accepted. There are also pessimists who argue that we have passed the point of no return and collapse is inevitable. I submit that we should learn the lessons of the last decades and recognize that neither the extreme hopes of the technological optimists or the extraordinary fears of the social pessimists will be realized. We shall continue to survive although the tensions which have required large expenditures on armaments will continue at high levels for the foreseeable future.

Internally, our central problem is still the same as has plagued us over the last quarter century. We have created a society based on countervailing power. We moved in this direction because it seemed unfair to allow certain groups in the society to control others. Today, when few groups are excluded from power, we have created a situation in which it is extraordinarily difficult for policies to be developed on a coherent and continuing basis because there is no agreement among the various pressure groups; fragmented adversary politics therefore dominate.

I am not suggesting that we should abandon our commitment to sharing power. I do believe, however, that we must look more realistically at some of the consequences which have followed from this effort to ensure fairness in the society. As we all know, different groups continue to espouse fundamentally different visions of the world toward which we should struggle. There are those who feel that we could raise the standard of living far more rapidly if we were willing to commit ourselves to this goal through the use of high technology.

Representatives of this group have asked me to make the following statement in my State of the Union message:

As you are well aware, there has only been a very slow rise in the standard of living in America, throughout the rich countries and indeed the world, during the last two decades. This situation has been accompanied by significant rates of inflation which have gravely damaged social fabrics.

We continue to believe that it is absolutely essential to use the potentials of high technology which exist throughout the various sectors of the economy. It is a sheer lack of nerve which prevents us from producing sufficient energy for all our needs. Only the fact that other countries have also suffered from a late–twentieth–century lassitude has prevented us from being in far worse shape than is now the case.

We need to set the economy free from the various shackles that have been placed on it. All around us we see evidence of creative imagination and will power, but we are like Gulliver bound by the Lilliputians. If you will curb the bureaucrats we can answer not only the crying needs of our own people but those in the rest of the world.

We recognize that our rhetoric is overblown, but we believe that the beginning of a new century is the time for our nation to relearn the obvious truths which we have ignored for the last two decades. Mr. President, in your last year in office you have an unparalleled opportunity to show what can be done, to succeed where President Reagan failed.

We know that you are under pressure from other groups. We have tried to work with them, but we have reached a stalemate. Only inspired government leadership can break us out of our present situation.

From the other side of this debate, I hear calls for a firm move toward a realistic recognition of the peril of our planet and the need to plan in terms of ecological limits. Representatives of this group have asked me to make this statement to you:

As you are well aware, the population of the earth is now at the 6 billion level and a further doubling is inevitable even if everything possible is done to minimize birthrates. At least a million people a year find a way into the United States despite our redoubled technological efforts to close the Canadian and Mexican borders as well as our seacoasts.

We are well aware that the standard of living has not risen in the last two decades. Indeed, figures calculated on a reasonable basis, rather than using GNP models, show a major decline. It is our thesis that this result is inevitable and will continue. Only if we transfer our attention from the quantity of life to the quality of life can we meet our needs in the future.

Even though we have been successful in holding down the extreme and absurd growth projections made in the early seventies, present patterns of ecological destruction are so serious that we must redouble our efforts to block further growth plans, and above all we must work against the extreme groups which are pushing for a return to belief in high–technology routes into the future.

Mr. President, we plead with you. At the beginning of this new century let us finally understand that humanity is part of the biosphere. Let us recognize that we may well be at the limits of what the biosphere will tolerate without rejecting us.

I could, of course, bring to this chamber other evidence of today's extraordinary splits. But you are as well aware of them as I am: indeed, that minority of you who will stand for a further term in the House or Senate are struggling to understand the cross-pressures.

Let me close by restating some of my own views. I wish that I could reintroduce the optimism of some of us who were in government in the early eighties. We thought that a new "management" pattern was being created which would break into the dangerous trends which seemed to be appearing. We thought that we might be able to restructure the society in appropriate ways which would open up new potentials for Americans and for all the rest of the world.

That hope was destroyed by the world's second great depression. It took all our skills to survive that crisis. Regrettably, insufficient thinking had been done to create effective change. We proved that it was possible for crisis to lead in unfavorable directions as well as favorable ones.

Looking therefore at the situation from my central position, and as one who is recipient of more pressures in the course of a day than it sometimes seems possible to manage, let me stress that I do not believe that either of the extreme views which I have reported to you earlier in this speech are either reasonable or politically feasible.

We have fought our way back from the abyss. The levels of endemic starvation in the poor countries of the world are once again at low levels although the areas of famine which result from destructive climate patterns continue to tax us to the limit.

We are once again making progress. We have invented new social institutions which have helped us to meet the needs of the society and to maintain the possibilities for a "free enterprise" style.

Voluntary service for young people—which now proves attractive to more than 80 percent of the population—has allowed us to care for people who need it, to manage the new biomass forests at reasonable costs, to restore the cities, to improve health and educational systems. While some fear that the "voluntary" system is becoming coercive because those who do not enter it will be deprived of various benefits later in life, this danger seems to me to be far less than the gains we are achieving.

We have managed to replace the need for much transportation through modern communication technologies. The remaining needs for transportation are being met, although less well than any of us would wish. For example, the requirement that no car shall be

13

driven with less than three people in it produces grave hardships to citizens in certain areas. But the replanning of our communities and the help given to permit people to move closer to their jobs through house swaps is producing favorable results.

Education is slowly becoming more relevant to life. There are more and more school systems which mesh learning and living in creative and imaginative ways.

But I would be the first to agree that the long–run future is far from clear. Another doubling of the world's population, which does seem inevitable, will further increase the pressure on our borders. Desires for higher standards of living may not be able to be met. There are, indeed, serious questions about the stability of our total ecology.

I come to you therefore with no great plans and no clear–cut message. We face a rapid aging of our population in the next twenty years. We have seen a worsening in the climate. We know that in a very real sense we have failed to come to grips with many urgent issues.

But we are still here. Some may say that we are only "muddling through." But it often seems to me that in a democratic society this is a compliment, rather than the insult which is intended.

What then do I hope from this election? Let us avoid high-blown rhetoric and unreasonable hopes and fears. Let us continue to do the best we can, to settle for what our resources will support.

I suspect that one hundred years from now a president will stand here and make a State of the Union message not too different from mine. Ladies and gentlemen, I give you the United States. Besieged by problems, we survive. Long may we continue to do so!

Wall Street Journal: Electronic Delivery Service—January 1, 2000

Every day last week, Jim Smith woke up and read his personally produced edition of the *Wall Street Journal,* which contained just the information he had ordered. Jim always reads both lead articles as well as what used to be our "center column." He has listed a number of firms with which he wants to keep up and also a limited list of stock market prices. He also has specified certain country interests and general concerns: these can, of course, be changed at will.

Just recently Jim has been considering changing his job, and he has asked for all the ads which might interest him, which are on file, and where positions are not yet filled. Last week twelve new ads were delivered to him over the breakfast table. When we talked to him yesterday morning, he told us that he thought he had found his new career opportunity. He will be working in the North Atlantic Weather Control Office, which has recently been expanding its operations dramatically, despite the rash of lawsuits that has plagued it in recent years because of the claims of various people that their interests have been damaged by its activities.

queries and comments

Why do we start a review of the last quarter of the twentieth century with this lead? Obviously, the electronic wizardry involved in this style of learning has become commonplace in recent years. Nevertheless, we tend to forget that there have been critical secondary and tertiary consequences which were not expected and are still not fully understood. For example, the movement away from a paper–based society to electronic storage of information can serve as a symbol of the changes in patterns which are enabling us to sustain a far higher standard of living than in the seventies, without overstressing the resources which are available to us.

The movement away from paper dramatically shifted the forestry patterns in the United States by allowing the use of far more land for biomass needs and recreation. In addition, and perhaps more critically, it dramatized to people throughout the world the possibilities of substitution through continued technological progress. The fears, and indeed paranoia, that had developed about the impacts of science and technology began to recede. The amount of money available for research and development began to increase in the mid-eighties, and we are now seeing the fruits of this change in consciousness.

Obviously, we have not yet recovered the years that we lost during the Neo–Luddite movement of the eighties, when many people echoed the thinking patterns of those people who smashed machines under the leadership of Ludd during the early nineteenth century in Britain. Several of the problems that plague us today would have been far better under control if we had used the seventies and early eighties to maximum advantage. Nevertheless, there is no doubt about the progress that we have made.

The fears and nightmares of the seventies and early eighties are now revealed for what they were—the classic responses which appear to afflict the human race at the end of each millennium. Our situation today is like coming out of the tunnel into the light. We see almost unlimited prospects. What are some of the reasons for this far brighter picture?

The Development of Technological Wizardry

We have already referred to the central evolutionary pattern in the technological area over the last twenty–five years—the impact of telecommunications and microelectronics on the patterns of information movement and decision making. It has proved possible for top management to regain control of decision making systems, to obtain accurate, up–to–date information, to involve the citizen in deciding on directions through instant polls, etc.

Tied into this new pattern has been the ability of microelectronic systems to take over much of the repetitive mental work of the culture. The "working week" and "weekend" have lost their distinctness as the need to use limited leisure–time facilities effectively has forced the development of patterns which ensure their use for the largest possible period of the year. The development of domes to provide "summer climates" during the extremes of winter has also been one of the important breakthroughs in meeting the needs of our increasingly leisure–oriented culture.

The acceptance of what would have been called pornography in the seventies as part of the culture has also been startling: the seeds of this development were, however, planted thirty years ago. The spread of pornographic material and later acceptance in the large cities of group sex showed the direction in which we were moving. It is now accepted that this is an appropriate way for many people to fill part of their leisure. As a related trend, families tend to survive for shorter periods, but the new technologies provide ways to deal with the custodial and emotional needs of single– and multi–parent children.

Central to the last two decades is the revolution in the energy picture. Only a few people realized in the early seventies that the high cost of fuels would inevitably result in the development of radical conservation measures and the creation of new types of fuels. The time scales for changes were drastically overestimated—the prospects for synergy between various scientific fields were not understood. It became clear by the mid-eighties that fusion was a feasible, low–cost technology, and the monopoly enjoyed by oil began to crumble in anticipation. We are now at the point where we can anticipate an effectively unlimited supply of energy: this will allow us to mine low–grade ores, where this is a necessity.

The other major energy development has been the solar space stations which actually had direct impact earlier than the fusion options. The contribution to world power needs became substantial in the early nineties despite growing fears of what could go wrong. Despite one significant accident, it is generally agreed that the benefits outweigh the risks

This availability of sufficient energy and the consequent "solution" of nonrenewable resource problems is less critical than once expected because we have developed the ability to substitute on a far larger scale than seemed feasible twenty years ago. We have substituted computer storage for paper, fiber optics for copper, decentralized sun-powered systems for electric power and distribution systems, etc. In addition, biology has redefined many problems and provided many possibilities.

We have found ways to limit dramatically the need for various scarce items such as fertilizer, pesticides, and water through computer-controlled monitoring of agriculture. This is just one example of the way that information has become a substitute for resources.

queries
and
comments

The Rising Income Floor

Probably the greatest surprise of the last twenty years has been the speed with which population growth has come under control. The breakthroughs were, as usual, technological. For example, ways have been found to limit the viability of male sperm so that conception is impossible if a male uses a skin implant; this implant is effective for a full year. The failure rate is miniscule and the side effects minor—although there have been some reports of nausea.

In the poor countries, there is still a feeling in many areas of the world that birth control is the responsibility of the woman. Here again extraordinary technological progress has meant that most women have possibilities available to them that are culturally acceptable. This does not mean, as we are all too well aware, that the tensions between the rich and the poor countries have vanished or can be expected to be eliminated in a brief period of time, but it is true that the end of the population spiral is now in sight.

The dramatic rises in the standard of living almost throughout the world, caused by a combination of slower population growth and more rapid innovation, have proved that fast economic growth, so often derided by liberals, is indeed the best way to pull up the standard of living in the poor countries. The gap between the very rich and the very poor is now perhaps wider than ever but the standard of living of everybody in the world has risen considerably. The only exceptions are what are sometimes known as the "international basket cases," which seem unable to move toward self-sustaining growth.

There is a growing recognition, of course, that a ceiling to growth will develop at some time during the coming century, but it is confidently expected that this level will not be reached until the standard of living throughout the world reaches at least the levels that prevailed in the rich countries in the 1970s.

Because of technological breakthroughs, both in the United States and the rest of the world, the prospects of famine have vanished finally from the face of the earth. The fears that the United

States might have to overcrop its land to feed the hungry no longer exist. The assumption that supply and demand forces could, indeed, prove effective in allocating land has been totally vindicated.

The Role of the Multinational

This revolution away from pessimism and toward real hope has been driven by multinational corporations which have proven to be the only force capable of breaking through national and international red tape and moving the engine of progress forward once again.

We reached this point because the conservative movement which manifested itself clearly in the United States in the mid-seventies burgeoned rapidly, supported by changes in other governments such as Britain. The fetters which had been developed to limit the capacity of business to do what should be done were steadily reduced throughout the eighties. By the nineties a great deal of economic freedom had been restored.

Freed by this development and encouraged by the new patterns of public opinion, business launched out once again both into research and development and into entrepreneurial activities. Theoretical and practical barriers, which had been thought absolute, were broken so that today we live in a time of euphoria which approaches that in any previous period of history.

Indeed this euphoria could be our Achilles' heel. Although the pattern of the last twenty years has been far more favorable than even the editors of this paper would ever have been willing to guess, it seems paradoxically appropriate to raise the type of questions which were seen as critical in the seventies and which we may be in danger of forgetting.

From the ecological standpoint, what are the limits to the capacity of the environment? The fact that we have not met any limits yet does not mean that we will not do so. We are today more aware of the long lead times involved in the appearance both of new individual health problems and environmentally systemic issues. The waves of innovation of the past years will certainly cause some new problems to develop.

The nature of the challenges confronting the human race is continuing to evolve with dizzying speed. To take one limited example, our bodily structures apparently are quite different when we are brought up with an adequate diet than in the past when most people had only just enough to eat. What does the combination of ever–increasing heights with ever–increasing leisure imply for the future? What about the insight that all foods may be carcinogenic?

The human race has always flourished on challenge. For a significant proportion of the human race, the possibilities have never been greater. But it would be irresponsible to fail to recognize that many people do not have the capacity to meet the types of challenges which now exist. Could this situation have serious implications for societal morale in the twenty–first century?

Present patterns seem set fair. But there are enough historians among our staff, who have cooperated in the development of this lead article, to cause us to worry about periods where dangers have apparently vanished. We would be interested in any letters to the editor which would inform us of the problems that might be hiding behind the sun.

But for the moment let us wish you a happy and prosperous twenty–first century in a world where there are at present no wars, no famines, no plagues. Let us hope that the Four Horsemen of the Apocalypse have indeed been banished forever.

queries
and
comments

Wall Poster—Green Forks Commune— January 1, 2000

As the new century emerges, I want to remind myself and others of the extraordinary victories that we have achieved in the last two decades which have moved us toward a sustainable, low-growth, limited technology world.

During the second half of the seventies, it seemed impossible that we were going to control the juggernaut of economic growth and rapid change. All too often, citizen reaction, as reflected by the media, to the impact of oil and gas shortages seemed to be a demand for high technology solutions. Pressures built up to achieve efficient ways to produce more energy, particularly through the use of coal and nuclear power.

Those who tried to point out the need to consider the implications of these patterns of behavior on local and national ecology seemed to be losing ground. The possibility of overheating the world and thus flooding huge coastal areas, the possibility of cooling the earth and thus causing a new ice age, the dangers of destroying the ozone layer seemed to us to be largely ignored both by those who made public opinion and by the average citizen.

I was one of those who struggled through the increasingly depressing dark days of the late seventies. But the tide changed with the major nuclear accident in Pennsylvania in the late spring of 1979 and the gas shortage of the same period. The arguments of those who defended nuclear power as an essentially riskless technology were shown up as the hollow shams they actually were. The nuclear option was, as a result, rejected by the American people.

This backlash against nuclear power fortunately carried over into all the high technologies. We began to recognize as a society that it was essential to cut back on the "insults" made to the environment. We saw that we had been going along the wrong route and that it was essential to move back to a closer contact with nature and to limit the size and the impact of the man–made environment on the human person.

The change was extraordinary and dramatic. By the middle of the eighties we were set firmly toward the concept of a conserver society. Political leaders were no longer able to push for high technology or high economic growth without committing political suicide. Pressures were toward the decentralization of power and the reintroduction of community decision making which, in turn, implied largely decentralized technologies.

As we all know, we did not find it easy to make the necessary changes in the society. The eighties were a time of great turmoil, both within the United States and many other rich countries, which followed the same route that we did. World patterns also changed dramatically as the United States ceased to consume as large a proportion of the world's resources as had been the case in the post-World War II years.

It would be pleasant to be able to say that we succeeded in anticipating the problems that emerged as we convinced people that they should use less resources. Unfortunately, as we look back on the patterns of the eighties, it is clear that our failures of understanding did cause much unnecessary suffering.

Much of this suffering developed from the fact that we were surprised by the speed and extent of the change in the culture: we were therefore not ready to cope with it. But, in addition, we did not listen to the knowledgeable people who were working with us and tried to warn us of some of the obvious secondary and tertiary consequences of the patterns that were developing. Nor were we as aware as we should have been of the depth of the sociocultural changes which were developing and the consequences that would necessarily follow.

For example, conserver society patterns turned out to be linked to stable family structures. Some people returned to industrial–era nuclear family styles and more people moved into extended families as the architectural styles and zoning laws of our society changed and it became easier for large groups of people related by interests—if not blood—to live together.

A more serious surprise for most of us was the way in which the economic system began to unravel when people started to buy fewer goods and services. We had not really understood the implications of the Neo–Keynesian economic system which was based on the requirement that most people should have a job. Within such a system, jobs would only be available if there was sufficient demand for goods and services. As demand fell off, job availability was inadequate to provide jobs to all who wanted them.

queries and comments

There were many crises—personal, geographical, and activity oriented—as we moved away from the industrial–era activities which tied people to the speeds and styles of machines and toward the neonatural communities of today, which operate on more organic time scales. Large numbers of extremely poor people were unable to meet their food, fuel, and housing bills. Indeed, as early as March 1979, the *Wall Street Journal* contained a lead article which reported on the number of people who were killed by the cold/starvation in the previous winter.

Today, we provide opportunities for work to all those who are willing—those who work have enough resources to live with dignity. We are still plagued with those who believe that the world owes them a living, but there are ever fewer places where they can hide and live without effort. We have of course changed the definitions of work—parenting is now seen as essentially a full–time activity.

Internationally, the picture is very mixed, of course. Just as the decrease in demand in the rich countries led to unexpected difficulties, so the decrease in world trade caused great disruption. However, the theories of Frances Lappé and others proved out in many cases: the decrease in demand from the rich countries freed up local economic potentials which existed in many of the developing countries once the depression of the eighties ended.

There are still a large number of countries with very serious problems. We now know, however, that it is impossible to solve the difficulties of communities other than one's own, let alone the problems of geographical areas other than one's own. It is possible to be aware of other areas' problems, but one can only help in ways that do not interfere in the natural feedback processes of nature and societies. This was the mistake that we made in the fifties, sixties, and seventies, and we are resolved never to move in this direction again.

There are some alarmists, of course, who are arguing that the end result of this approach will be to cause the more desperate countries to decide to take over North American resources. I do not believe that this result is probable; but there are people who want to join Canada, Mexico, and the United States together in a mutual

21

defense pact. There would fortunately be extraordinary difficulties in implementing this proposal given the degree of decentralization that now exists.

Fortunately, however, I believe that there has been a continuing decline in the impact of ideologies, and an ideologically based conflict between various parts of the world now seems almost impossible. People throughout the world are so well aware of the difficulties that we have in staying within ecological bounds that fights about theoretical questions seem impossible. It seems extraordinary, from today's vantage point, that the primary concern of many analysts at the beginning of the eighties was the fear of a war between some unpredictable combination of the Russians, the NATO bloc, and the Chinese.

What then of the future?

I am personally satisfied with where we are today because we have made so much more progress in the last twenty years than I would have believed possible. I cannot be as nervous about the next twenty–five years as some of the younger people are. It all too often seems to me that they are creating problems rather than perceiving them. But I do teach young people, and I do recognize that their worries are real to them.

Last week, I asked some of our interns to write an essay for me on the twenty–first century—here are some of the quotes:

"Our community is very crowded and so is the world. Where am I to find the space that I feel I need?"

"We have been told by those who have lived through the last twenty years that we are using far less resources than in the past. I cannot believe it—we all seem to be so wasteful compared to what we could live on."

"What is the point of life? What are we meant to do with our existence? Why is it worth making an effort every day?"

"The Asian people have been asking for part of the North American continent because they are so much more crowded than us. They argue that it was our failure to help them to reduce birthrates at the same time as we reduced death rates in their countries that got them into their present precarious situation. As I try to be a leader in the twenty–first century, what is the right response?"

"Everybody says that we don't use high technologies. But I do not think this statement is true. Surely we should either get closer to Mother Nature again or we should recognize how much we still depend on high technology and take advantage of the inventions of the last twenty years."

queries
and
comments

I suppose that it is the last comment that shocks me most. I thought that I had convinced my students of the validity of the directions in which we are moving. Did I fail? If so, where did I go wrong?

Your comments on this wall poster are solicited. Please message me through the teleconferencing system—number 227—and I will respond to you.

A happy new century to you!

Terran Communication Council, January 1, 2000 (File + Get, Mark, 2000 Evaluation)

Like many other people, I have been trying to write up my perceptions of the world as we enter the twenty–first century. I'm offering these summary perceptions and ideas to those of you who know me because you have asked about my feelings.

As you will remember, I was fortunate enough to get an Orwell Fellowship in 1984. These fellowships were founded in gratitude to Orwell for his body of work and particularly his book *1984.* He forced us to think about the dangers of high technologies, particularly in the area of microelectronics. As a result of his warnings we were far more effective in searching for the positive potentials of these technologies. A couple of years ago, I joined the Terran Communication Council which is responsible for improving knowledge throughout the world and thus enhancing our capacity to make effective decisions.

The success of the Terran Communication Council is based, of course, on the understanding that decisions must be made on sapiential grounds—i.e., must be based on competence and knowledge rather than on power and position. As you will certainly remember, the shift away from power models and toward competency models in the eighties and early nineties created enormous tensions. This style does now seem to have been largely accepted.

But there are still dangerously high tensions in the world as we try to resolve the problems which developed because of failures of decision making in the period between the end of the Second World War and the beginning of the eighties, when the process of positive change became visible and effective. We have still not overcome the widespread deprivation—and limited starvation—in the poor countries although there are some viable reasons for hope for the first time.

Birthrates in the poor countries of the world have dropped very rapidly in the past twenty years. This change was due to technological breakthroughs, particularly in the area of male contraception, and also to more creative meshing between the cultural norms of various societies and the birth control technologies made available to these cultures. In addition, the socialization and reward process of most of the poor countries has been changed so that it accepts and benefits small families.

The drop in the birthrate has also permitted us to get ahead in the educational area for the first time. Throughout the sixties and seventies, in the vast majority of the developing countries, each generation of children was less well educated than the previous one. Now we can see a significant improvement in the competence of young people, and definitions of competence are also changing rapidly.

There have been several reasons for this improvement, besides the decrease in pressure because of a less rapidly growing population. First, it is no longer assumed that the Western industrial–era model of education will necessarily be appropriate in the poor countries. It is increasingly understood that the education/socialization process must fit the realities of each particular area's situation. This better mesh between the specific needs of each area and the styles of education used has greatly increased the potential of most human beings.

Second, we are using microelectronic and communication styles—particularly those in the oral mode—on a continuously intensifying basis. Critical to this change have been the patterns of knowledge restructuring, such as the problem/possibility focuser, developed by the Terran Communication Council.

Now let me list some of the changes which strike me most as I look back on the period since I was born in the early sixties:

—The concept of personal and community growth has largely replaced that of "economic" growth. We have realized that the economic statistics on which we previously set such store were highly biased and created serious distortions in the decision–making process. We now look at measurements different than those we used in the past, and we are interested in resources primarily as they help or hinder our processes of individual and community growth. (From my earlier comments, you know that poor countries still face critical resource issues.)

—Our growing ability to do more with less has been critically related to the abolition of the distinction between the "week" and the "weekend." Work and recreational resources are today used as intensively as is feasible without arbitrary time distinctions. Thus, schools and churches, office buildings and theatres, fishing and hiking trails are far more appropriately managed. (While we have moved to abolish arbitrary time distinctions, we are, however, far more conscious of the need to work with daily, monthly, and annual personal energy cycles.)

—People who were born a decade or two before me still feel that their life styles are heavily restricted by the reduction in personal mobility that has occurred during the last twenty years. Most of us no longer feel justified in taking long–distance vacations, except under exceptional circumstances, as the cost in nonrenewable resources is too great. Perhaps I should add that people born when I was, or afterwards, find it difficult to understand why people want to move around so much because we hate to leave our friends and our community. When we have to move our places of work we find ourselves adapting to new community styles with great difficulty.

—There is today much greater movement in and out of leadership roles in the society than there was in the past. It is now considered pathological for a person to dedicate himself or herself to service for the society for their whole lives. Rather, people move into and out of leadership roles in a far more flexible way than has ever previously been the case. As a result, we have found that the leadership pool is far larger than we had ever believed.

—Pressures to keep oneself healthy have greatly increased in recent years. In most communities irresponsible behavior likely to damage one's self or others is unaceptable. This style sometimes threatens to move over into "coercion," and there are crucial worries about this danger in certain of the health problem/possibility focuser groups. But the improvements in health patterns have been so great that almost everybody feels that the gains have been worth the cost up to the present time.

—The increase in community pressures to maintain one's health is felt by most people to be more than counterbalanced by the decrease in the pressures around the legal area. By the end of the seventies, the fear of lawsuits was a major constraint against any form of creative action. The dangers of being sued had increased to the point that many people were not willing to take on social responsibilities. However, a reverse move to replace legal action with arbitration and mediation had been quietly gathering strength and burst out in the eighties.

—Interestingly, I find that I have so far left out the incredible changes in the economic system over the last twenty years. We, of

queries
and
comments

25

course, no longer operate under the Keynesian model which forced up consumption in order to provide jobs for all. Today, the system is worked from exactly the opposite end. We ask how much resources are needed for the operation of the society. We then try to ensure that people will do the minimum amount of toil and also ensure that people spend the greatest possible part of their lives doing the things which they believe are important for themselves and for their communities.

—We have learned to understand the conceptual differences between renewable and nonrenewable resources. We are more and more careful of those resources which, once used, are lost. We have, on the other hand, made extraordinary strides in growing and developing our renewable resources. The productivity of our forests has been rising at a 3 percent rate over the last twenty years and the rate has been increasing rather than declining.

In addition, and critically, we have been able both to preserve significant wilderness areas in various parts of the country and to augment the effectiveness of joint use patterns. We are now reducing our needs for oil and gas at a pace which should ensure a relatively painless transition to a solar/biomass strategy. However, many of the issues around the importance that should be given to the high–technology model, as opposed to low–technology, decentralized styles, have not yet been resolved. For example, the first solar space station which beams power down to earth has been completed and works, but we have not yet decided whether it is a desirable model for the future. On a related issue, questions are once again being raised about the amount of resources which should be used for deep–space exploration; it is argued that now that we are able to work with each other on a sapiential basis there may be enormous advantages in going out into space in a cooperative style.

If an observer from the seventies were jumped to this beginning of the twenty–first century, I suppose that the most dramatic changes would be:

1. Extreme poverty does not exist in the United States, although some people still manage to waste resources to such an extent that they are quasi-destitute.
2. Polls show that almost everybody sees himself as having a *higher quality* of life than that of a decade ago although people recognize that they have *fewer goods and services* available to them.
3. Energy use is significantly lower than it was in the late seventies despite the increase in the population.

Now let me try to guess what a member of the Terran Communication Council looking back on us from the year 2025 might say in terms of our successes and failures:

queries
and
comments

1. Significant progress had been made by the year 2000 in developing a world management system. The creation of the Terran Communication Council still seems an almost miraculous event even from our perspective.
2. In 2000, there was far too little understanding of the implications of the dramatic aging of the population that would take place between 2000 and 2025 in the rich countries and between 2025 and 2050 in the poor nations.
3. While discussion had started by the year 2000 of the need for meshing logic and intuition in education and management, little real progress had been made in setting up effective systems.
4. Even the Terran Communication Council did not recognize in 2000 how much movement of the world's populations between continents would be needed. The large in–migrations from the overcrowded regions of the world to North America, Africa, and Australia—the world's remaining open spaces—produced new strains on social fabrics.

As you will see, I think that we are still at the beginning of our challenges. But we have come this far, and we have turned some corners that previously seemed impossible. This should surely give us the courage to continue.

As always, I'd love to get your reactions to this document; message me here. The work that I am now doing makes these perceptions critical to my work, and if they are wrong, I urgently need to correct them.

3 Driving Forces

You will have reacted to the biographies and scenarios according to your current perceptions of reality. Some of the material will have seemed more realistic and other parts more acceptable to you. Some of you may be so dissatisfied with all of this material that you will want to write something of your own before you go on to consider the driving forces that will demand change during coming years.

Our period in history is unique because humanity is now powerful enough to change the world. This is true not only for the new weaponry which is now so destructive that it could effectively erase all life from the planet but also for our ability to change ecological systems—both as a result of conscious decision making (as in the case of the Aswan Dam) or through unexpected feedback as in the case of acid rain or the DDT chain.

The material here aims to help you to deal with these questions by setting out some of the primary driving forces which are operating in the society at the present time. In order to make it easier for you to carry out this exercise, you should imagine yourself in the following situation: You are a member of a futures staff working on American problems and possibilities for a powerful consortium of foundations. You have just received a memo from the head of your group which reads as follows:

This material represents the results of the work that we have done following the request of the task force that we consider which driving forces are likely to be the most intractable in the next two or three decades. We are looking for those forces to which the United States must *adapt* because of a lack of control rather than those that the United States may be able to affect significantly through good decision making.

The foundations want to meet with me next week to discuss these forces in terms of an effort which they are considering to inform the American people of the new national and international context. At our last session we decided as a group that we would present no more than nine subjects—we did not want to overload any eventual educational effort. We also left out the weaponry issue and the survival questions since they seemed to all of us to need to be tackled using a significantly different approach.

The subjects that we have decided to include are:

1. *Tensions Between the Rich and Poor Countries*—Obviously this problem is going to be a major part of the international context which cannot be changed.
2. *Population Changes*—The "bulge-in-the-snake" phenomenon is only now beginning to get the attention it deserves. Few people understand how significantly this will continue to disrupt the overall structure of the United States over the next fifty years.
3. *Migration Factors*—The migration from North to South and East to West is now well established and will almost certainly continue for much of the rest of the century. The shift from urban to rural areas is only now taking hold and will, given people's desire to escape the cities, almost certainly be a significant force for two decades.
4. *Ecological Balance*—The environmental consciousness which grew up in the 1960s, and burgeoned in the early 1970s, is now under increasing attack. The realities of the situation, however, are that any significant cutbacks in commitments to cleaning up our environmental problems will threaten the health and long-run safety of our population.
5. *Energy/Resource Availability*—While it may be possible to obtain enough resources for a long time into the future, costs will be far higher. Increasing costs will force significant infrastructure shifts, and it may well be impossible to maintain all the present capital stock. To take one example, the road and bridge situation is becoming critical in many parts of the country.
6. *Telecommunications*—Although we have agreed that decisions about the level of technology are to a considerable extent cultural ones and will vary with American attitudes, there appears to be one exception to this rule. The technology of telecommunications will continue to develop rapidly because there is no real opposition to it at the present time, although different groups hope that it will be employed for different purposes.
7. *Changing Knowledge Patterns*—The world both *is* more complex because of the greater speed and intensity of worldwide communication and it also *seems* more complex because we are internalizing the idea that everything is connected to everything else. Thus the management structures that can be effective need to be reconsidered.

29

queries
and
comments

8. *Climate*—We have had many discussions about this issue with competent meteorologists and among ourselves. We have found no clear-cut evidence of heating or cooling trends, although the theoretical possibility of both exists. But we have discovered that there is rather general agreement that the climate in the twentieth century has been unusually benign and few feel that this will continue— indeed, there is much argument that the pattern is already worsening.

9. *Biology*—The next dominant issue after the computer and microelectronics evolution is clearly the impact of the biological revolution. Man is not only going to be able to create various life forms but he is going to be able to control the direction of his own evolution. Can we develop the wisdom to cope with the extraordinary powers which are already in prospect?

I know that some of you still have ideas that you think should be included.

I would welcome your proposals for replacements of one subject with another. However, given our time limits I must get completed drafts from you. In completing these proposed documents, do not forget the distinction between driving forces and social issues which has confused us in the past. We are defining a driving trend as one over which there is likely to be relatively little policy control—a social issue as one where intelligent policy choices can be expected to have a significant effect. I also need your suggestions for changes in the existing drafts. What should be taken out and what should be added?

Finally, I hope that you will continue to develop your personal scrapbooks of items that either are directly relevant to a driving force or throw a peripheral light upon it. You have your loose-leaf manuals available to you for this purpose, and we are now developing computer linking techniques. The new ideas that have developed as a result of linking items which usually remain separate continue to amaze me.

Let me stress that there is no agreed list of the driving forces that will make change inevitable. Nor are there firm divisions between driving forces and social issues. For example, I have excluded economic affairs as a driving force in the belief that we can and must change our system so that we do not continue to be whiplashed by the desire to minimize both unemployment and inflation. Others, of course, would see economic growth as *the* critical driving force.

1. Tensions Between the Rich and Poor Countries

It is now almost thirty years since the well-meant efforts of the rich countries unbalanced the socioeconomies and cultures of the poor countries. Those working with the poor countries were appalled at the unnecessarily high death rates and decided to reduce them.

In some areas the decreases in the death rate were almost incredibly rapid: for example, in parts of Southeast Asia. In other areas, the decline was slower. But the results have been similar throughout the world, and the gap between birth and death rates has been wide in most parts of the poor world for several decades.

The historical balance with both high birthrates and high death rates was thus broken. We are now in a position where, if major catastrophe can be avoided, rapid population growth will continue in many areas of the world for at least a further quarter of a century.

What Could Be Done?

There is increasing understanding that rapidly rising populations are gravely damaging development prospects in many parts of the world. But arguments about the effective steps to take vary widely.

The conventional wisdom still appears to link the standard of living with desired family size and to argue that a fast enough rise in income can be achieved to cut into the rate of population growth. This model is based on a parallel with the patterns which developed in the countries now rich. The difficulty with this model, of course, is that we have been trying to raise standards of living over the last thirty years, and we have only been successful in a few countries; it is not clear where breakthroughs will come in coming decades to ensure a better record and thus a reduction in birthrates.

There is an alternative school of thought about ways to control population growth which has considerable underground strength although it is not "respectable" and gets little public attention. This school proposes that we set the "nonviable" countries adrift and leave them to shift for themselves. It is highly probable that this style of thinking will gain strength as problems get more acute. This concept should be resisted not only on moral grounds but also because systemic analyses of the consequences show that the effects of such a move could only be disastrous for the citizens of the United States.

The hard truth appears to be that we have not yet been willing to look honestly at the realities of the rich-poor split, how long it will be with us and how serious it is. While there may be shifting alliances among the varying countries of the world over the next decades as perceptions of national interest change, it seems inevitable that tensions between the rich and the poor countries will intensify for at least a decade. This reality lay behind the platitudes of the Cancun conference in the fall of 1981.

The Causes of Tensions

Because the West sees the world in largely economic terms, Western analysts created a new conceptual model following the OPEC embargo. They suggested that we should see the oil-rich countries and the other poor nations as totally different. The events in Iran should alert us to the fact that this split is all too often misleading.

The dominant force in many poor countries is not economic benefit but values and culture. The conflict of ancient vs. modern is being seen in all its intensity in Iran: one of the primary splits may turn out to be between the "liberated" woman and the Ayatollah. It goes without saying that present differences build upon older tensions but, in effect, the fabric of the society is being torn in many directions. The classic revolutionary "steps" have developed but at a far more rapid pace, presumably due to modern communications. We can anticipate similar problems in Mexico.

In effect, therefore, the influx of large amounts of money through the sale of natural resources may well speed up the process of culture shock rather than alleviate it. This implies that the countries on which we are relying for materials may well be the most vulnerable to cataclysm. This may have implications for national policy which are far deeper and wider than we have yet realized.

We must cease to attribute the causes of instability primarily to the machinations of other world powers. Events in the poor countries are not being driven by the communist/capitalist split but by "future shock." Only when we learn to get inside poor country realities might we be able to develop a set of tactics and strategies which are responsive to poor country needs.

One Clue to Thinking and Action

We need to look closely at the process of cultural and socioeconomic adaption which is now taking place in the poor countries of the world, and to do so in the context of America's changing needs.

In the fifties and sixties it was assumed that the development process of the poor countries would inevitably follow that which took place previously in the countries now rich. We have so far tried to convince the poor countries to learn and use the strategies which had brought us to our stage of affluence. Today, we are becoming aware that rich countries have been moving in some wrong directions.

We now know that it may be possible for the poor countries to skip certain of the stages of growth that were necessary for the countries now rich. For example, it is increasingly suggested that communications may make the development of a high-level road transportation network undesirable and unnecessary.

At the cultural level, it is being suggested that both the agricultural era and the new era we are now entering need to be fundamentally cooperative. The industrial era, as we well know, has been competitive. We should work with the poor countries of the world to see how the cooperative structures they inherited from the past can work for them in ensuring the transition from the agricultural to the communications era.

... the momentum of the long-term trend toward utilitarian, rational, industrial society would continue bringing us a future that would be a continuation of the past, but plagued with increasingly vexing social and environmental problems. A third dilemma confronts the technologically and industrially advanced world: We cannot risk the international instability that results from the vast disparities between the rich and poor nations, yet neither of the obvious solutions—making the poor nations richer or the rich nations poorer—seem feasible. The world probably cannot afford to have the gap closed through making the poor nations as productive, consuming, and polluting as the rich nations; at the same time, the rich nations are not likely to choose voluntarily to become less materialistic and more frugal. We often assume (with considerable justification) that the most probable future is a direct continuation of past trends. Yet it is apparent today that many long-standing trends cannot continue unaltered: World population cannot forever expand exponentially; world energy use cannot increase endlessly; patterns of world mineral consumption must change. In fact, it has been apparent for several decades that modern society has broken with the past in a number of important respects.

—Willis Harman.

queries
and
comments

... the age of chivalry is gone. That of sophisters, economists, and calculators has succeeded.
—Edmund Burke. 1729–97.

Our Western way of life is marked by excess—
excess of consumption,
excess of accumulation,
excess pollution,
excess waste,
excess destruction,
excess armament
excess use of resources.

We are being made to expect too much.
We are taking too much.
We are scrapping too much.
We are paying, and compelling others to pay, too high a price.

and so now we are saying
ENOUGH IS ENOUGH!

We call upon you to consider your resources and your needs, your life-style and your stewardship and, together with us, to reshape our personal, social and national priorities.

We ask you, together with us, to ask, again and again, this question: Will this purchase, this change, these plans make our relationships more fruitfully human in the context of our own one human family?
Will this enrich or impoverish the personal values of other people?
Will it clarify or cloud people's awareness of themselves as children of God?

Do we still dare to ask such questions?

—Leaflet, based on John Taylor's *Enough is Enough.*

2. Population Changes

The high birthrates of the late fifties and the early sixties are going to create major perturbations in the social and economic climate of the United States during the next fifty to seventy years. This result is certain, although there is still great disagreement about what many of the impacts will be.

The Post–World War II Baby Boom

Births peaked at 4.3 million in 1957, were 3.5 million in 1968, and have been in the range of 3.1 to 3.3 million for the period from 1973 to 1979. Regardless, therefore, of future birthrates, which could rise significantly, there will be major consequences from what has been called the bulge in the snake—the large population cohorts born in the late fifties and early sixties as compared to the figures for earlier and later years.

The major impacts have so far resulted from the decline in school-age children. Many schools have closed; teachers find it increasingly difficult to get jobs; there have been considerable increases in juvenile crime; unemployment rates among young people are, today, very high, etc. Colleges are now feeling the impact of the decrease in the size of population cohorts. Many believe that a significant number of colleges and universities will close in the eighties.

What will happen as the bulge in the snake moves onwards? During the eighties, the largest population cohort will be in their twenties. From the optimistic point of view, this will lessen the need for additional jobs, will decrease juvenile crime, will increase productivity as people get used to the world of work. But there also are likely to be "unexpected" results: primary among them will be the extraordinary difficulty of providing well-trained and educated people with tasks worthy of their skills. The consequences of this underemployment can only be guessed at today, but it must surely increase job-related tensions. The efforts of women and ethnic minorities to secure good jobs are already seriously threatening white males. The issues which surfaced in the Bakke case must necessarily become ever more difficult to manage. These difficulties will increase still further in the nineties and the first decade of the twenty-first century.

Not until the second and third decades of the twenty-first century shall we face the problem of a population which has an unusually large number of old people.

Indeed, the short-run problem of the aging of the population has been exaggerated unless there are breakthroughs in longevity. Looking at the range of U.S. Census Bureau predictions, the proportion of people over 65 will only rise from 10.7 percent to a range of 11.3 percent to 12.9 percent in the year 2000. On the other hand, there will be a substantial shift in the average age of the population from 29 years now to a minimum of 32.5 and a maximum of 37.3 at the same date.

If age-specific birthrates should hold constant over the next decade, there will be a substantial rise in total births in the eighties. How large an increase will develop depends on cultural forces which lie outside the scope of this briefing paper. It is essential to remember, however, that the highest Census Bureau projection would result in a birthrate a full 1 million above the historical fifties peak. The median Census Bureau figure would bring us back to the 4.3 million range of the late fifties.

The Impact of Immigration—Legal and Illegal

It now seems reasonable to hope that the pattern of world population increase which started in post–World War II years as the rich countries helped the poor countries reduce the death rate, without dealing with birthrate issues and without anticipating the consequences, has reached its maximum percentage rate of increase. Unfortunately it seems *impossible* that the absolute rate of population increase has yet reached its peak—only the development of war, famine, disease, and pestilence on an extraordinary scale could alter this reality.

Given the gap in wealth between the poor countries and the rich—a gap which will be maintained and reinforced by differential birthrates—there will inevitably be attempts by individuals to move into the rich countries, legally and illegally. The central and immediate problem for the United States is obviously the Mexican border. New dynamics will emerge as Mexico becomes an oil-rich nation. The prospect of a major crisis resulting from immigration over this border seems very great. There are peculiar secondary consequences of this situation—for example, the attempt to get an accurate census count for the United States will be complicated by the fear of reprisals and related sets of issues. (The differential birthrates for various ethnic groups within the United States will also have a destabilizing effect on political patterns with "Spanish-speakers" expected to become the dominant minority.)

Given the fact that the rate of immigration, both illegal and legal, is now a significant factor in U.S. population dynamics, there is clearly a need for a reexamination of what immigration goals are feasible and desirable in today's conditions. The combination of the nineteenth-century hope of "give us your huddled masses yearning to breathe free" with the actualities of today has resulted in muddled thinking, confused policy, and growing feelings of guilt. For example, and specifically, it will probably become technically feasible to "close" the Mexican border: should we do this? The Cuban and Haitian exoduses of 1980 have brought closer the moment when we must deal with these questions.

Now Nettie, not another baby is my peremptory command, two
will solve the problem whether a woman can be anything more
than a wife and mother better than a half dozen or ten even.
    —Letter from Susan B. Anthony to Antoinette Brown,
April 22, 1858.

queries
and
comments

The Green Revolution has not brought any significant respite
from hunger and malnutrition in Asia. Despite a total of more
than 50 million acres planted in high-yield varieties of rice and
wheat, grain production fell to dangerously low levels throughout
Asia last year.

The main problem with the miracle seeds is that they are
engineered to outperform native varieties only under the most
favorable ecological conditions and with the aid of enormous
amounts of industrial fertilizers, pesticides, insecticides,
fungicides, irrigation and other technical inputs. Without such
inputs, the high-yield varieties perform no better—and sometimes
worse—than the native varieties of rice and wheat, especially
under adverse soil and weather conditions.

Even when the technical inputs are applied in sufficient
quantities, certain ecological problems arise, which seem not to
have been given adequate consideration before the seeds were
"pushed" out into the vast acreage they now occupy. Conversion
to high-yield varieties creates novel opportunities for plant
pathogens, pests and insects. The varieties also place
unprecedented stress upon water resources. . . .

Of course, every man-made technological disaster has its
man-made technological solution. But the peasant smallholders
of Asia cannot meet the costs of spiralling technical inputs
needed to avoid disaster. The Green Revolution inevitably
widens the gap between landowners who have the credit and the
know-how to keep up with technological solutions and the
peasant smallholders who stand to lose their land when the
unanticipated ecological side effects appear.
    —Marvin Harris.

Given the changing role of women in society people expect them
to have a career. But many women find they have no economic
or other incentive to develop a second career after their children
are out of the nest, and so, for a few, having another child is a
career. For that kind of parent sometimes there's a real need to
help the child free himself from that parent's terrifically
child-oriented involvement with him.
    —Janece Kline.

37

queries
and
comments

3. Migration Factors

A basic sociological theory argues that massive migrations are often one of the primary causes of dislocations in a society. According to this thesis, the migration from the rural areas to the central cities and from the central cities to the suburbs in the forties, fifties, and sixties has created serious disequilibria which we are still trying to resolve.

Many federal government policies are directed to managing the sets of problems which resulted from these past migrations. Large amounts of money flow into the central cities in an attempt to cope with obviously critical problems. But too little has been achieved.

While the dominant demand of the cities is still for more money, some mayors and town managers are showing greater sophistication in terms of what might be really helpful. For example, many cities and states are ready to accept *less money* in order to have *more control* over how it is spent. Similarly, the federal government is looking for ways in which it can work with communities to ensure that *overall goals* are met rather than *specific program requirements*.

North–South Migration

But while we concentrate on the effects of past migrations, some totally new trends are developing which are causing new stresses and strains that require far more attention than they are yet receiving. In recent years, the movement from the North to the South has grown so rapidly that magazine issues have been developed with titles such as "The New War Between the States." There is still considerable conflict not only about the meaning of the trends but also about the ways in which growth statistics should be interpreted. Northern states tend to argue that the income and resources gap between the North and South is almost closed and that there is now need for a more evenhanded policy, while the Southern states argue that there are still major differentials.

It is our belief that we are in urgent need of a "nonconflict" model for this discussion. It seems highly probable that both the Northern and Southern states would benefit from measures which would begin to slow movement down. The costs to the North in the present situation are obvious. But the building and facilities costs to the South at a time of rapid increases in costs are also very significant. As a result, there is growing evidence of changes in power structure views about the desirability of growth in states such as Arizona which have experienced rapid growth.

East–West Tensions

A profound split in attitude has developed between the Eastern and the Western states. This split could be significantly aggravated by the fact that the resource base of the country is moving toward the west.

queries
and
comments

Further, the boom-town/boom-area problem must be expected to complicate policy making in coming decades. The need for considerable outside help in boom-town areas has been established, but success in setting up institutional arrangements to help with needs has so far been limited.

Urban–Rural Migration

The boom-town/boom-area problem is part of a far wider issue which is still largely unperceived by the American people and their policy makers. During the seventies a very significant reverse flow from the metropolitan to the nonmetropolitan counties had started. It is estimated that 3 million people have moved into nonmetropolitan counties between 1970 and 1976. This is the first time that such a development has been recorded in American history.

There is no agreement at the present time as to the significance of this trend or why it is happening, but here are some reasons we have discovered as we have been studying the picture:

—According to the polls, Americans have wanted to leave the cities for a long time; today they seem to be acting in terms of their desires.
—The cities have become ever more expensive while the rural areas seem to promise lower living costs because in the country it is possible to avoid building and other standards which are often more strictly imposed in the cities and suburbs.
—It is increasingly possible, using the new telecommunications technologies, to be effective working in the knowledge industries in the rural areas. (This last factor is still probably a minor one but we believe that it will grow in importance with the extraordinary telecommunications breakthroughs inevitable in coming years.)

The harsh reality, however, is that without an order of magnitude increase in the amount of help that is made available within the rural areas, there will inevitably be major breakdowns in the capacity to govern them. There are a number of institutions which could be mobilized to help, such as the Cooperative Extension Service and the land grant universities, but much work would be required to reorient and revitalize these institutions for a task of this magnitude.

39

Value Systems

In addition we *must* not transfer urban styles to rural areas. The attitudes and values of the rural areas are still surprisingly different from those of the towns, and it is critical that new programs be designed to fit the real needs of the inhabitants of the nonmetropolitan counties. Only a major creative and imaginative effort can hope to ensure gains rather than losses as the necessary help is provided.

Let us close with one example of the magnitude of the problems. It now seems almost certain that the statistical styles and patterns we use today are not effective even for the purposes for which they were designed. It follows that they are particularly inappropriate for the rural areas. We need to imagine and create totally new statistical techniques. Thus while there is a need for money in the rural areas, providing too much will simply attract a new breed of consultants rather than encouraging communities to start working with and for themselves, which is the only way that effective solutions can be found.

The French Revolution's Declaration of the Rights of Man listed among innate and inalienable human rights the liberty to stay and to move freely. Vigorous political and economic liberalism removed the barriers against immigration and emigration . . . together with other barriers to human activity.
—Encylopaedia Britannica

We speak of today's America as still a society of mobility. It is. There are people moving up, down, and across hierarchies. People do move from one city to another, from one house to another, even from one occupation or sometimes one religious denomination to another. But ours is a special kind of mobility. Its special character is not remarked on because, we suppose, it seems to be totally natural. That character is of being fixed in a kind of partialized, exclusive unit before and after one exercises the right of mobility.
—Robert E. Agger.

This is a fascinating poll. This is a big vote for extreme caution on growth. People have been telling me for years that Arizonans are very environmentally conscious in the broad sense of that word. I still find that somewhat surprising.

I've always thought that people here were hell-bent for growth at any cost, an attitude which I don't share, but which I thought was the dominant attitude. While I do find it very surprising, I am equally glad to see it.

I think I would read behind this, "Look we're concerned about deterioration in the quality of life, of the things that brought us here in the first place. We know that growth is inevitable. We don't oppose it, but we're very skeptical about whether or not we can manage it any better than Southern California did!"
—Bruce Babbitt, commenting on a poll of 3,200 people in Arizona.

queries
and
comments

4. Ecological Balance

It is sometimes argued that the success of the ecology movement in the sixties could not have been anticipated because it cut across the basic drives of the American culture. But such a statement fails to understand that there has been, throughout American history, a desire to maintain the integrity and the beauties of the land. Many struggles between economic growth and ecological protection have been won, by any means, by those supporting the most rapid rate of economic growth.

The pattern today is confused. Is the ecological movement fighting a rearguard action to preserve the gains it has won or is the public still solidly behind it? The polls are not helpful in answering this question for, depending on the types of questions which are asked, it is possible to prove anything that one wishes using various surveys.

Indeed, this question as it is normally posed is hardly worth considering. The correct policy question goes far deeper and is far more difficult to answer. We need to consider the points at which the environmental degradations associated with economic growth are so serious that they must be controlled.

It is already clear that conceptual errors have been introduced into the legislative process and that these will have to be reversed. The process of reversing past errors will be seen by some as an abandonment of the ecological cause. For example, the idea of zero pollution is simply infeasible for many products and processes—the only way to achieve it would be to shut down the process or product. (This same problem is now critical in the food and drug area where it is increasingly suspected that overdoses of [almost] any product will be carcinogenic.)

How is Balance to be Achieved?

How are we to balance the needs for production with valid ecological concerns? Today, we are coming to suspect that the "lim-

queries
and
comments

its" beyond which irreversible environmental damage is caused cannot be determined scientifically but only through experience. For example, there are scenarios which suggest that major heating or cooling in the atmosphere would result from slowly growing concentrations of various pollutants or an increase in the heat generated by combustion. The point at which change would be triggered cannot be determined with certainty because we do not know (probably cannot know) enough about the earth's atmosphere to simulate the processes.

In considering these issues, we need to remember the reality of discontinuous functions in man-controlled activities and also in nature. One of the classic examples of a discontinuous function occurs in connection with freeway flow. The slowing down of cars on the freeway is not a straight-line function connecting number and speed—rather there is a point at which a dramatic slowing takes place with the addition of a very small number of vehicles.

Natural processes behave in the same way. It follows that we must necessarily be cautious in our choices if we are to be certain that disastrous consequences will not develop. This type of thinking will necessarily be threatening and unacceptable to groups who argue that we should continue maximum rates of economic growth until we have resolved some of the most serious of our worldwide socioeconomic problems.

Any belief, therefore, that ecological concerns can be abandoned in this country and the rest of the world fails to understand fundamental ecological reality.

New Forms of Conflict Resolution

If this is indeed true, then we are going to have to create significantly different models for conflict resolution. Today, federal legislation can be used to delay activities which are found objectionable by any specific group. The most obvious path uses the environmental impact statement, but there are many other methods of bringing a particular project back and back for reexamination. This results in rapidly escalating costs which we pay as a society and individuals—costs that add significantly to the inflationary spiral.

We need fundamental rethinking. This should start from the statement that it is possible for the United States to meet the cost of the needed environmental programs. On the other hand, it is not desirable for the United States to pay the costs required by some legislation. In addition, citizens should not be forced to pay for the costs of continuous discussion and litigation.

Our essential problem is philosophical. It is still assumed by our legal and political processes that society can gain enough knowledge to create an absolutely correct decision. Thus, each time a new fact or piece of data emerges, it is assumed that this implies that the "correct" decision may not have been reached. Obviously, given bad faith on any side, the situation rapidly becomes intolerable.

We need to develop a fundamentally new pattern for making decisions about difficult, controversial, and potentially damaging questions. We need to find ways to draw together all those who are affected by and have skills to help resolve a particular situation. We must then make decisions on the basis of the best information that is available at a particular time. After the decision is made, there would then be an extremely strong presupposition that the issue had been closed. Reopening should only take place with an extraordinary strong justification, and the rights of those who acted on the assumption that a final decision had been made should be respected and, if changes are made, there should be compensation. Such a model would begin to restore some stability to directions.

We are, of course, suggesting very significant changes in legislation, thinking, and values. But we believe that there is now sufficient evidence about the costs in time, and in individuals' and institutions' willingness to commit themselves to significant activities, that changes of this magnitude are urgently required.

We are not suggesting here that the scales should be tilted toward or away from economic growth or environmental balance: this is a far broader issue. We are only suggesting that it is in the interest of all of our society that we find ways to reintroduce some certainties into our political and socioeconomic system.

This we know.
The earth does not belong to any man; man belongs to the earth.
This we know.
All things are connected like the blood which unites one family.
All things are connected.
Whatever befalls the earth befalls the sons of the earth. Man did not weave the web of life, he is merely a strand in it. Whatever he does to the web, he does to himself.
This we know.
—Chief Seattle.

In today's world all curves are exponential. It is only in mathematics that exponential curves grow to infinity. In real life they either break down catastrophically or they saturate gently. It is our duty as thinking men to strive toward a gentle

saturation although this poses new and very difficult problems.
—Dennis Gabor.

The main problem is that, in view of the political immaturity abroad today, it is unlikely that mankind will earn survival without a major disaster. If we are more realistically optimistic, we can envisage that in the next 200 years the oceans will be a disaster—today even the remotest beach has patches of oil on it. The continents will be devastated, and only 100 million human beings will still be around on Earth. The main terrestrial life form will be insects.
—Jacques-Yves Cousteau.

We must realize the importance of communication and of understanding each other's social, economic, and political differences. We must share an awareness of the need for balance as we consider what the future will be.

When we talk about economic development we think of balance. We know we don't want to scatter smokestacks across our state, jamming our open spaces that make us so attractive now. But we know that people cannot enjoy open spaces without jobs provided by economic development.

When we talk about energy policies we think about balance. We believe we have a potential with our resources to become less dependent on outside sources for energy. But we are not going to recklessly pollute our air or rip up any more topsoil to meet what has become an almost insatiable energy appetite. We see the need for a balanced transportation system and are working on it.
—Robert D. Ray.

5. Energy/Resource Availability

One of the most confusing and heated arguments of the present time is about the availability of energy and resources. Part of the problem emerges from different estimates of the amount of minerals, etc., in the ground. More critical, however, are the different conceptual models that are used.

On the one hand, there are people who argue that we have always managed to find reserves when we need them and that it is therefore reasonable to expect that we shall continue to do so. On the other hand, others state that it is inevitable that we shall be forced to use lower and lower grade resources and that, as a consequence, costs will rise. Eventually the costs of extraction will, according to this model, exceed the benefits.

This debate can fortunately be resolved using basic economic theories which have been around for over a century. The British economist Ricardo proved that land economics and product economics are not the same and that it is a major error to treat them as though they are.

queries
and
comments

Differences Between Production and Resource Economics

In normal supply and demand economics, when a product becomes scarcer, the price rises. This increase in the price then increases the attractiveness of creating more of the product, and after a short or long lag, the consequent increase in supply will normally bring the price down again. Whether the new price, after the change in demand, is higher or lower than before depends on complex interrelationships between the elasticities of demand and supply. It is, however, almost certain that the short-run rise in the price will be larger than the long-run rise.

In today's conditions where prices are largely controlled, supply and demand patterns work less freely than in the past because fewer goods and services are subject to market prices. But the basic tendencies remain, and it is always true that an attempt to force a price above the "equilibrium level" will cause counteracting forces to develop, both as people buy less of the product and as others try to find ways to supply it or to invent alternative goods and services which can substitute for the need.

Most economists and businessmen seem to consider that the energy and nonrenewable resource situation is similar to that which exists for goods and services. To a certain extent this is true: there will be decreases in demand and increases in supply as the price of a nonrenewable resource does rise. For example, some analysts point to recent rises in the price of copper which made mining different types of ore attractive. This caused a slump in prices.

It is this pattern on which Norman Macrae of the *Economist,* and others, rely when they forecast a glut in energy supplies in the eighties. They suggest that the activities of a large number of people, all considering their own self-interest, will cause a fundamental change in the situation. For example, new technologies seem to promise very large increases in gas mileage and very large increases in the capacity to recover oil from wells which previously yielded slowly or were no longer yielding at all.

Paradoxically, however, real successes along these lines—successes which may be occurring now—might well be the worst thing that could happen for the long-run survival of the human race on this planet. This is where we have to look at economics more carefully.

Land and Resource Economics

The key point made by Ricardo was that the supply of land was finite. He was aware that a small amount of land could be added to the stock and that the efficiency and effectiveness with which land was used could be changed. But in the main, he argued, the amount of land available could not be significantly changed.

Thus, he pointed out, when the demand for land went up, there was no chance of any significant increase in the supply. The increase in demand would therefore inevitably push up prices and the payments to landowners would increase more rapidly than the amounts of money available to labor and capital, the two other factors of production.

This pattern has, of course, been developing throughout the world. In Japan, for example, the prices of all land have reached fantastic levels. Costs have also been increasing in the United States recently and, indeed, in all the rich countries. There is, as a result, an increasingly popular theory that one of the primary causes of inflation is the very significant rise in land prices throughout the world which then become incorporated in all other prices.

How does this theory relate to the resource issue? Nonrenewable natural resources behave similarly to land in economic terms. It is for this reason that many of those concerned with resource use are arguing that we should immediately take steps to limit usage so that those generations which come behind us will have the maximum opportunity not only for survival but for living in the best possible conditions. These arguments have so far not dominated our socioeconomic debate.

While one of the reasons for the lack of acceptance of these ideas is that they challenge deeply rooted behavior patterns, it should also be noted that there is an intellectual rebuttal to resource conservation. Thus, the argument has been made that we shall become intelligent enough to find totally new types of resources such as "anti-gravity," the ability to use the sun directly, etc. It is then stated that we both can and should use the now-useful resources of the earth prodigally at this point so that we can build a "bridge" to the period when we have become "gods" and are able to set up a high-level, self-sustaining socioeconomic system.

There is no effective way to compromise between the various arguments which are advanced by different groups, for they emerge from completely opposed visions of the way the world works and should work. People write fundamentally different scenarios for the future based on these varied views.

We are the ciphers, fit for nothing but to eat our share of earth's fruits. It is not the possessor of many things whom you will rightly call happy. The name of the happy man is claimed by him who has learnt the art wisely to use what the gods give . . .
—Horace 65–8 B.C.

This statement is written in the recognition that mankind is at a historic conjuncture which demands a fundamental reexamination of existing values and institutions. At this time three separate and mutually reinforcing revolutions are taking place:

The Cybernation Revolution: A new era of production has begun. Its principles of organization are as different from those of the industrial era as those of the agricultural. The cybernation revolution has been brought about by the combination of the computer and the automated self-regulating machine. This results in a system of almost unlimited productive capacity which requires progressively less human labor. Cybernation is already reorganizing the economic and social system to meet its own needs.

The Weaponry Revolution: New forms of weaponry have been developed which cannot win wars but which can obliterate civilization. We are recognizing only now that the great weapons have eliminated war as a method for resolving international conflicts. The ever-present threat of total destruction is tempered by the knowledge of the final futility of war. The need of a "warless world" is generally recognized, though achieving it will be a long and frustrating process.

The Human Rights Revolution: A universal demand for full human rights is now clearly evident. It continues to be demonstrated in the civil rights movement within the United States. But this is only the local manifestation of a worldwide movement toward the establishment of social and political

regimes in which every individual will feel valued and none will feel rejected on account of his race.
— Ad-Hoc Committee on the Triple Revolution.

Consider the Ferret—

The Black Footed Ferret, whose last stronghold is South Dakota, is unable to exercise any control over its environment and is on the decline. Tilled fields have displaced the once superabundant prairie dogs which are the ferret's prime food resource.

Some energy resources, once thought limitless, now have known exhaustion dates. The dates may be years in the future but nevertheless have a grim finality. It is up to us, mankind, to exercise control and make the most efficient use of our resources together. Efficient use slows depletion ensuring that economical alternative energy production methods for electricity will be ready well in advance of the time existing fuel sources are exhausted. In the Black Hills we have an adequate supply of energy to use, even to share, but none to waste . . . use what you need efficiently.
—From an advertisement series of the Black Hills Power and Light Company.

There is endless merit in a man's knowing when to have done.
—Thomas Carlyle 1795–1881.

6. Telecommunications

Throughout the post–World War II years, the drive toward microelectronics has continued with remarkably little societal attention to its short-run and long-run effects. Although its effects have remained "invisible," microelectronics will clearly be one of the most important and critical driving forces in the United States and the world over the rest of this century and into the twenty-first.

It may be revealing to look first at the reasons for the lack of visibility of this force which has already transformed our lives through the hand calculator, the computer, and the growing flexibility of communications systems. What has hidden the effects of this extraordinary force from the general public?

Issues of *Science* and *Scientific American* published in recent years both commented on this relative invisibility but failed to explain the reasons for it with any great success. Here are two possibilities. First, we are used to perceiving change in terms of buildings and structures, but the very nature of the telecommunications revolution limits the need for structures. In fact, the development of fiber optics, microwaves, and satellites is making the cost and visibility of communications developments even less than in the past.

Second, and perhaps more critically, no group in the society has so far believed that its interests are *severely* threatened by the development of microelectronics. Different groups tend to look at the potentials it raises for them while ignoring many of the dangers. There have, of course, been some limited concerns about privacy and "big brotherism," but these concerns have so far been marginal, although they may well increase in the future.

Support comes from various groups for different reasons. Those who believe that high technology and high economic growth are the route into the future are convinced that only more sophisticated equipment, which must of course include computers, can permit the continued increase in supply which is essential. In addition, microelectronics is seen as the only way to increase productivity in many areas of the economy, particularly in "service" trades.

Those who believe that low technology and low economic growth are the route into the future do have some limited fears about computers, but this is not normally a priority issue for them. Indeed, the conserver movement is itself divided on this subject: there are a large number of people who believe that the best way to cooperate between communities, and also permit individuals within communities to work together, is through a computer-based teleconferencing system.

Others believe that computers can improve management systems in very significant ways. This group is interested in the new styles for structuring knowledge made available through more flexible and cheaper computers and the connections between them.

Probable Directions

We are doubtless going to see the rapid development of microelectronic technologies. The only certainty is that the consequences will be startling. For example, there is growing discussion of the paperless office, and while it may well develop less rapidly than is sometimes assumed, it will have a major impact on the consumption of paper by the end of the eighties.

Why is it so difficult to get a fix on the likely directions of the microelectronic revolution? In part, the problems emerge from the very speed of development in the field—there is a saying among those most closely involved that if you go away for a month you may well miss a generation of equipment. While this statement *is* exaggerated, there is an important grain of truth in it.

In part, the problems of analysis emerge from the fact that the microelectronics technology can be used for so many different purposes. For example, the home video recorder can be used for improving education and to support a wild explosion of pornography. The video disc and cable television, the more effective automobile and teleconferencing, the giant computer and the personal computer—and much more—all stem from this explosion of knowledge.

It is for this reason that the discussions now going on in Congress about the future of the telecommunications industries—indeed the knowledge industries—are so critical. People have obviously not yet understood that the historical divisions between computers and telephones, television and home entertainment centers, cable and network television are steadily being whittled away by the progress of technology. Attempts to prevent competition between these various areas through regulation are therefore doomed to failure, although these attempts may cause considerable confusion. Similarly, the effort to preserve the monopoly of the post office or the cable companies for the sending of messages is like Canute trying to hold back the tide—the primary negative result will be to slow down the emergence of technologies and styles of decision making which would help to manage our present crises.

The search for new ways of communication is another characteristic of the present. This development can be considered peculiar to our abundance era; indeed, the situation develops because of a super-abundance of "information."

This overabundance of information causes saturation; saturation then leads to blocking, and the blocking disorients the thinking of men and societies. These processes of blocking and disorientation are visible at both ends of the society. At the bottom, the question is posed in terms of the coherence (and even the existence) of societies which are no longer controlled by will and design but appear to have developed their own dynamic. At the top, the question is one of power—those holding it seem to vacillate between a belief that they can impose order and an understanding that they cannot control the system which has now developed.
—Georges Gueron.

The free flow of ideas worldwide is needed if mankind is to solve the approaching global crisis of increasing population, pollution and dwindling resources. Marshall McLuhan understood the pivotal position of media in our time before most of the rest of us did.

—J. Edward Murray.

queries
and
comments

7. Changing Knowledge Patterns

In recent years, there has been increasing discussion of the ways in which fundamental changes in patterns of thinking and organization of knowledge take place. There is now widespread agreement that the process takes the following form.

Knowledge structures come into being because they are found effective at a particular time. Because no knowledge structure can be complete or explain *all* the phenomena that confront it, exceptions to the overall structure will inevitably be found. The knowledge structure is then stretched to accommodate the exceptions. As time goes on the exceptions become so large a part of the total pattern that the underlying organizing simplicities with which the structure started are almost lost to view. At this point, the search starts for a simplified model. If and when this is created, it may be adopted with "startling" speed.

Alternatively, the ideas which could support a new model may remain "invisible" for a significant time before the society is willing to consider them seriously. In this case, as in all others where creativity is involved, the choice of the proper moment is crucial. For if the society feels that it can still get by with the old theory despite its flaws, it is unlikely to submit to the vast upheavals which will inevitably be forced by the introduction of a new knowledge structure.

One of the primary intellectual questions today is whether we are indeed undergoing what is known as a paradigm shift: i.e., a fundamental change in perceptions. More and more people argue that changes are taking place and that these profound alterations in thinking styles will be one of the primary driving forces in the society over the rest of the century. We agree with this belief, although we know that there are still strong voices raised against this conclusion.

What is the nature of this new paradigm? What will it imply for American and world society? This is one of the questions which we *should* be considering at the present time if we are to have any reasonable prospect of avoiding world collapse. In considering this question, however, we need to distinguish carefully between the understanding that is possible of the forces that are driving us and the results that will follow if these forces are able to work themselves out.

Let us use a physical analogy. It is now possible to state the vectors which are driving us and the directions in which we shall move. But we cannot hope to know what will be the final shape of the society once these vectors have worked themselves out.

Today's changes parallel those which occurred with the evolution into the industrial era. There were, at the beginning of the industrial era, a limited number of people who perceived the driving forces which lay behind the industrial system and the directions in which society would change. However, practically nobody was able to perceive the types of social, economic, and political models which would develop as a result of these forces.

What then are the central elements of this new paradigm and how do they differ from the fundamental understandings which underpinned the industrial era?

1. There is a growing understanding that "everything is connected to everything else" and that analysis of part of a system without consideration of its interconnections is extremely dangerous. This implies that the disciplinary pattern of understanding that underlay the industrial era is now a cause of very significant error.
2. There is a growing understanding that it is impossible to act in a system or even to observe it without altering it. This implies that the belief in an "objective" world, in which truths are absolute and unchanging, is now a cause of very significant error.
3. There is a growing understanding that all decisions involve the balancing of uncertainties and risks. Our present social sciences—which either ignore or minimize the consequences of risk—are now a cause of very significant error. (It is not generally known, for example, that conventional economics has no theory of risk at all.)

The new paradigm takes these three critical realities into account. The most important conclusion which emerges is that there can be no absolute and immutable truths. The truth can only be found by comparing and contrasting various perceptions of reality as seen by different people who have had different life experiences and therefore necessarily understand their world in different ways.

This pattern implies, in turn, that we must develop love/trust relationships and win-win systems. Such systems are *essential* be-

queries
and
comments

cause people will not dare to share their fragile visions of the truth with others unless they are convinced that they will not be laughed at or taken advantage of because of their statements. (It is for this reason that the decline in trust throughout our society has such crippling results.)

The implications of this new paradigm are much broader, of course. How do we develop and make available knowledge when we can no longer state absolute truths? What sort of documents and knowledge systems are required when we admit that all we can do is to state partial and contradictory views as honestly as we can. These views then serve as a basis for ongoing dialogue in our struggle toward the truth.

Many of those who do believe that we are in the middle of a paradigm shift argue that this implies that we live in an ahistorical period. There have, of course, been paradigm shifts in the past, but the speed at which this paradigm shift must take place if we are to survive—i.e., within a single generation—is totally new.

Past paradigm shifts have taken place as the old have died off and the young, with new visions, have taken their places. The present paradigm shift will require each citizen to rethink his own hopes and fears for the future and to work with others to achieve the most favorable results for all those involved.

I am not an advocate for frequent changes in laws and constitutions, but laws and institutions must go hand in hand with the progress of the human mind. As that becomes more developed, more enlightened, as new discoveries are made, new truths discovered and manners and opinions change, with the change of circumstances, institutions must advance to keep pace with the times. We might as well require a man to wear still the coat which fitted him when a boy as civilized society to remain ever under the regimen of their barbarous ancestors.
—Thomas Jefferson 1743–1826.

We must regard ourselves as transitional men, not men of the past. As transitional men we have a place—as a link between the age that is ending and the new, and often, mysterious one that we are entering. I believe we have the vital task of ushering in the new era. It is our task to make available those traditional values which future generations may need. We must not be hurt, however, if our values are sometimes rejected.

Few generations are privileged to usher in a new age. The hunting tribes who first started farming were one such

generation. The farmers first to form a city-state were another. The Renaissance commercial giants of Florence, Sienna and the Hanseatic League were another. The great industrialists of Britain's 19th century were another. Now we are challenged, in my opinion, to join these privileged of history. Only together shall we be worthy of our time in history.
—Patrick Hartt.

Can we diversify without becoming trapped in contradiction, build a pluralistic society that will be able to maximize personal development and move beyond material abundance? Can we construct a society that will respect all persons and their diversity, and will be able to cope with the coming crunch of population (six to seven billion by the end of the century)? These billions are the ones who will undertake a rethinking of philosophy, ethic, and organization.

In hoping that humanity succeeds in this collective task, let us be cognizant of the risks we run and, calculating the effects of failure, pay careful attention to the conditions for success. Should wisdom and tolerance become practical civic virtues instead of being the exclusive property of "great" men? Does our future depend on this?
—Georges Gueron.

8. Climate

We have less to say on this subject than on other driving forces, but we are so convinced of the importance of this issue that we believe that it must be kept in mind whenever we discuss the future of the United States and the world.

We have had a large number of discussions with climatologists. There are at least as many theories as there are climatologists. These theories range all the way from close-in trend analyses to those that seem to partake primarily of science fiction. We have also taken note of the popularity of a recent novel which deals with the triggering of a new ice age, and we remain thoroughly uncertain that any one person or group knows the truth in this area.

It is obviously possible that man's activities could at some point be of sufficient magnitude to affect the climatic patterns on earth. On the other hand, it can also be argued that humanity's total efforts for the foreseeable future will be trivial compared to what the earth can do in terms of hurricanes, earthquakes, eruptions, and other similar natural patterns.

As one looks back at the geological record, it is, of course, clear that there have been major changes in the world's climate over time. It is also clear that we have neither the knowledge nor the power at this time to reverse such a major change if it should begin to develop. The more appropriate question with which we must deal is whether we can learn enough to avoid triggering a catastrophic alteration through our own actions. Our skills and knowledge are still so limited at the present time that the only possible intelligent decision would seem to be caution wherever there is any evidence of a significant danger. Questions of what we mean by "significant" and the ways to measure "significance" are controversial and will become more so: one example is the ozone layer issue.

queries and comments

Apart from these long-run, "catastrophic" changes, there is one other climatological concern which deserves attention. There seems to be considerable agreement that the basic climate of the last fifty years, both in the United States and on a worldwide basis, has been remarkably stable and benign. In other words, there have been less extreme climatological events than the norm, and the patterns of weather from year to year have stayed remarkably "stable." (It may be difficult to believe this statement because the weather each of us experiences often appears as a series of extremes.)

If the forecast of greater climatological variation is correct, there would be very significant problems in the near future. Agricultural innovation patterns of the twentieth century have concentrated on improving yields within narrow ecological niches: this pattern has worked only because the climate has fluctuated within a relatively narrow range. If there should be a major shift, then the yield of many varieties of crops would drop precipitously because of the fact that they were so narrowly adapted.

A similar problem might emerge with diseases and pests which could increase dramatically because of changes in climates. The monocultures throughout much of the United States could provide ideal conditions for propagation of such pests and diseases.

We suggest three actions:

1. Alerting the American people to the importance of the climatological issue. This might prove an ideal area for education. It would inevitably teach the complexities of decision-making, for discussions of climate inevitably require an understanding of probabilities.
2. Allocating enough resources for intensive discussions between the most competent climatologists in order to determine what are the reasons for their disagreements at the present time. Efforts should be made to broaden patterns of

agreement and to narrow down the causes of disagree-ments. We are excited by the new patterns of knowledge, creation, and transfer which have been developed for these purposes.

3. Making sure that this subject is covered effectively in any conference which you may decide to call to consider driving forces.

Like other nature-related risks such as earthquakes, our ability to predict climatic changes is minimal. Predicting any future risk is difficult at best, but in the case of climate, that difficulty is com-pounded by gaps in our knowledge of the workings of the climatic system.

Left to her own devices, Nature will gradually slide into the next Ice Age. It is due over the next 10,000 years. But many climatologists believe that something unnatural may be happening on the way to the next deep freeze—and it is happening now, not in thousands of years from now. The peculiar factor influencing the climate is *people,* who through their industrial and agricultural activities are competing with natural processes that determine climate. . . .

While it is clear that very few of the questions about future climate-related risks can be answered with precision, it is equally clear that some decisions cannot be postponed until very precise information is available. One example is whether to continue burning fossil fuels. Such combustion, which produces carbon dioxide (CO_2), will likely affect the climate. . . .

The menace of CO_2 lies in the fact that it tends to absorb infrared radiation, trapping some of the earth's heat which normally escapes to space. This has been dubbed the "greenhouse effect"; it is analogous to a greenhouse in which the glass allows solar heat in but blocks its escape to the outside.

The greenhouse effect of CO_2 could raise global mean surface temperature about 1°C by the turn of the century and by 2–3° by the middle of the twenty-first century. These seemingly insignificant changes are sufficient to disrupt the earthly heat balance and approach the magnitude of the average global temperatures from warm epochs to the Ice Ages!
    —Stephen H. Schneider.

9. Biology

This is the next great revolutionary force which will hit us after telecommunications. Its implications are, of course, potentially far more pervasive than the implications of the telecommunications revolution, for the biological revolution may change our whole vision of what life is, how it can and should be created, and to what degree it is sacred.

It is indeed difficult to know where to draw the barriers around the biological revolution. Does one consider the ability to provide artificial insemination? Or the social change which would follow if we decide to adopt the suggestion, which has already been made, to breed from Nobel Prize winners? Or the growing ability to test for birth abnormalities, thus increasing the pressure on parents to make difficult choices for or against abortion? Or the ability to determine the sex of children before birth, which in a still more permissive society than ours could lead to children being aborted until one of the right sex was conceived? Or more effectively, the division of sperm so that the choice of sex could be made at the time of artificial insemination?

We have become used to selective breeding of plants and animals. Interestingly, experts are now less certain that the results have all been beneficial, for there is a wider understanding of the trade-offs which are involved. The questions become far more critical, of course, when one starts to consider breeding to achieve a "better" human being. What does one mean by "better" in these circumstances? Who should be the ideal?

What about the idea of lengthening the life span? Is it feasible? And would it be desirable? What about the concept of freezing people so that they can survive until cures for their diseases are found? Or, on the other side, what about the questions raised by a right to death?

Even negative eugenics—the concept of breeding out dysfunctional patterns caused by defective genes—may contain more risks than are generally recognized or may be acceptable. We know very little about the linking of various genetic patterns: asthma is something one might want to get rid of but would one lose empathy also? Dyslexia—an impairment of the ability to read—may possibly be tied to high intelligence.

But all these issues are peripheral as compared to the possibility of developing new life forms in the laboratory. This potential has already been demonstrated at low levels through recombinant DNA approaches, and it is expected to develop rapidly. The potential dangers so impressed those involved that special controls were devised and later largely dropped, but nothing can be more certain than that these will be bypassed and circumvented as firms try to make a profit in this field.

Nobody knows what could happen. Could a germ develop to which human beings had no natural immunity? Are there any chances of a new organism emerging which would take a dominant place in the environment? At this time there is little certainty as to what will be science fiction and what science fact.

One reality is already clear. It will not be possible for politicians to write legislation that is appropriate. A problem that has been serious in previous changes will become critical. Who will advise? How will those who advise be chosen? How will all legitimate interests be safeguarded? And who will watch the watchers?

This is not the only driving force for which such questions are relevant. But these questions are particularly important in this field of biological engineering. Indeed, it may well be that the process of managing change itself may be a more critical problem that any of the specific areas where new ideas are required.

Will mankind have enough sense to preserve the complexity and diversity of nature which may be necessary to induce, and to continue or preserve, high human intelligence? The current rate of heedless homogenization of the world's once diverse environments is not encouraging. The transformation of *natural* diversity into cornfields, cow pastures and concrete cities on a world-wide scale appears almost inevitable. Yet, concurrently, the marvelously interesting *cultural* diversity of the world is being obliterated as well. Eventually, human intelligence might well degenerate into stereotyped responses to the few stimuli allowed to survive.
—Hugh H. Iltis.

As a member of society, it is necessary for a biologist now to redefine his social obligations and his functions, particularly in the realm of making judgments about such ethical problems as man's control of his environment or his manipulation of genes to direct further evolutionary development.
—Encyclopaedia Britannica.

4 Social Issues

Society is today being largely driven by inertial forces. The changes which are developing are those which are dictated by the impact of these forces rather than those brought about by creative activity. The central issue which now faces us as individuals and as a society is whether we have the courage and the imagination to alter our socioeconomic system before the dynamics presently built into it destroy us.

One critical problem we face is the failure of the media to bring information about the new world which surrounds us to the attention of the general public in ways which would permit them to understand it. There are several reasons for this failure. First, public affairs programming is traditionally considered so dull that people do not normally watch it; the exceptions to this generalization seem to be designed to create heat and not light. Second, there is considerable unwillingness to break through the conventional unwisdoms and to consider new realities.

To dramatize the social issues discussed here, the material is set out in terms of a letter suggesting possible television programming. To give you latitude, you can choose any role in which you might have received this letter. You can think of yourself as the head of a network who has received a letter from a former colleague. Or think of yourself as somebody in middle management receiving a letter from a subordinate. You can choose to operate in the commercial or the public broadcasting sector. You can think of yourself as a White House official who has asked for a proposal in this area. Here is the letter you have just received:

Dear Mr. Smith:

As you will remember, we have talked several times about the possibility of creative television programming which would enable the American people to understand more effectively the types of issues which are going to emerge in the eighties. We have both regretted the fact that there seems to be no way in which it is possible to reach large numbers of people through patterns which will enable new thinking to take place.

I have been so concerned by this apparent reality that I decided to write up a proposal so that we can decide whether the position is as hopeless as we have tended to assume in our on-again, off-again conversations. I must admit that as I have developed this material I have come to believe that it would

queries
and
comments

indeed be possible to create suitable programming. I therefore await your reactions hopefully.

Let me start by restating three of the assumptions which we have talked about together and which underlie the rationale for this effort:

1. There is growing conflict between the goals of various people and groups in the United States. This conflict, unless it is better understood, is likely to lead to increasing difficulties in decision making. Thus, meshing the desire for equity and the drive toward economic growth may well need different sets of policies today than in the past. Similarly, educational policies and the styles of jobs which will be available in the future may also be out of phase. Examples of this type of conflict can be multiplied many times.

2. The conventional wisdom assumes that people in the United States are not ready to consider fundamental change. This viewpoint is certainly supported by some of the polls which have been taken in recent years. But there are contradictory polls which show a willingness to look at totally new directions. What are we to make of this evidence?

3. In our conversations, we have suggested at various times that there is a gap between what people really believe and what they *think* they "should" say or "can afford" to state within their role models. I have told you about some of my positive experiences. I have been able to work with groups in far more fundamental and creative ways than their public image would appear to make feasible.

I am convinced that there is already a felt personal and community need for better information. There is also obviously an urgent need for more complete knowledge if governmental systems are to remain viable. What then is the block to new styles of television programming and other styles of information movement? I believe that it can be relatively easily identified.

We all know the figures which demonstrate the precipitous decline in trust in various institutions—and those who represent these institutions—in the United States over the last fifteen years. We remember, less often, the inevitable corollary of this situation —that people are unwilling to believe the statements of leaders who they are sure have failed to level with them in the past. Any TV programming, based on information which emerges from these distrusted people and institutions, is essentially doomed to failure before it starts. It cannot possibly receive the fundamental attention which it must have if it is to affect significantly established dynamics in the United States.

This would seem to bring us to a dead end. Fortunately this is not the case. Several people and groups have been trying to discover new ways to structure knowledge. The new styles they are creating make it possible for individuals to understand the differences which exist between the views of various people and groups on a specific subject and to help them to understand the reasons for their differences.

I am arguing that it is essential for any programming on these fundamental issues to accept and clarify the existence of very different views on topics and the reasons for these disagreements. I am convinced that it is only in this way that the general public will make the effort to try to learn the complexities of our present situation. People are now highly confused by the different points of view that are being advanced and they want, above all, to learn new ideas to enable them to make sense of these apparent disagreements.

Some time ago on the "Good-Morning America" show, David Hartman asked two senators how each of them and the president could confront the same set of "facts" and reach such different policy conclusions. Similar pleas to help the public understand the reasons for differences are heard more and more often. We could effectively help the public with new programming using the problem/possibility focuser approach.

What sorts of subjects am I suggesting we examine? Here are some ideas placed in random order.

1. *THE BABY BOOM ECHO*   The number of women in childbearing ages is continuing to rise and will do so throughout the eighties. This has not so far caused a large increase in the number of births. Will this situation continue; or may new trends develop which will cause people to want more children or less? Will rights to abortion be limited? This program could help people understand the interconnections of economics, values, attitudes, and birthrates. (I have set out each of these social issues at somewhat greater length in an appendix to this letter, but I am summarizing here so that your colleagues may have a shorter document to which they can react.)

2. *STYLES OF EDUCATION*   As you know the "back to the basics" siren song continues to be heard in the land. It is certainly having some effects; many of these seem favorable to people who grew up in the industrial era. The ques-

tion which we would need to take on in this program is whether the basics for the twenty-first century are the same as those we teach today. (I wonder if mothers with children being born this year realize that their children will not enter college until the twenty-first century.)

3. *LEVELS OF MORALE* Is it possible for a society to function with present levels of morale? What could be done to bring back trust? Do we need truly different patterns of knowledge and leadership than we have had in the past?

4. *ACCEPTABILITY OF HIGH TECHNOLOGY* Obviously the citizens of the United States are being whiplashed between those people who feel that only high technology will save us and those who fear its consequences. The recent problems with nuclear power have obviously made the issues far more acute. What are the real options open to use in a world with 4 billion people now and at least 10 billion before population stability is achieved?

5. *THE POLITICS OF ECONOMICS* We have accepted the Neo-Keynesian economic mode. It has worked very badly for us during the past decade; but there has been no effective challenge to it except the monetarist challenge, also from the past. Where are the new economic thinkers? Given the nature and extent of the challenge, why have there been so few significant new ideas? Or have there been new ideas and the transmission belt to the public is missing?

6. *LAW OR MEDIATION/ARBITRATION* It is clear that we have become a litigious society. Why? Is this pattern tied, as many people believe, to the decline in trust, the feeling that one has probably been cheated and one should get compensation whenever one can? If this is the case, how could the trend be reversed? Are there real possibilities in the field of arbitration and mediation, or are they chimeras?

7. *EQUALITY VS. DIVERSITY* We have been moving toward a more equal society for a long time. Now a backlash is developing against the idea. Did we misinterpret the idea of equality? What can we learn from the Bakke case? What lessons should we learn from the fact that ecological systems seem to need diversity? Does this mean that human systems need it also?

8. *LEVELS AND STYLES OF DECISION MAKING* We are very well aware today of the demand for more local autonomy. However, there are also people who believe that more centralization is essential for the effective running of the United States at the present time. We can expect to see

very tense discussions, and, probably, confrontations around this issue in coming years. We need to look at the world differently—how can people be introduced to this idea successfully?

This letter has already run on too long. But I must add that it will not be enough simply to produce and air these shows. We would have to encourage a whole series of locally based efforts if we are to reach people effectively. I hope that you can make suggestions as to the ways to do this, building on previous follow-up programming efforts.

I look forward to an early reply.

Sincerely yours,

Jane Brown

Appendix to Letter to Jim Smith—Attachment

The Baby Boom Echo

We are now becoming aware of the consequences of the peak in births in the late fifties and the early sixties and the subsequent decrease so that the birthrate in the seventies has been consistently more than a million below the peak level. This "bulge in the snake" is going to lead to constantly changing social priorities as different age groups become the largest one in the population.

We have, so far, spent little time looking ahead into the eighties. The number of people in the childbearing ages has been rising consistently throughout the seventies and will continue to increase throughout the eighties. It will decline again toward the end of the century. There has not yet been an important rise in the annual number of births because marriages have come later, a significantly larger percentage of people than in the past wish to remain single, and desired family sizes are far lower. (In analyzing birthrate patterns, it should be remembered that there are still a large number of teenage births, including illegitimate teenage births, and that far more young unmarried mothers are deciding to keep their children rather than making them available for adoption.)

What is going to happen in the eighties? The number of births is already rising—the real question that needs to be considered is the extent of the rise. Let us look at some of the forces that may affect the birthrate.

1. The cost of bringing up a child continues to increase. This is a substantial disincentive for a number of people. If a recession or depression should develop, the desire to keep down the number of children will be even greater.
2. Birth control and abortion information is far more widely available, although there are widespread cultural pressures to reduce this flow of information.
3. There has been a rise in "hedonism" in the seventies with more people looking toward their own personal gratification rather than thinking about how they can help others. As the raising of children is costly in terms of effort and time taken away from one's own personal desires, this attitude tended to lower birthrates.
4. There has been, at the same time, a loosening of family ties because industrial-era styles have split parents and children as they grew up.
5. The religious base for the family has been eroded over the last century, but this pattern shows signs of reversal.

The impact of many of these factors may be in the process of changing significantly, possibly dramatically. Certain scenarios for the future would lead to a far more fundamental religious approach to life, in which the joy of family living might again be extolled. In addition, the mobility of the industrial era seems certain to decline as the cost of energy compared to other goods and services continues to climb. In addition, many women have put off having children and a "bunching" of births is a real possibility.

We might consider dramatizing this issue by showing different types of possible family life in the nineties. We could ask viewers to vote for which seemed most and least attractive to them. It would be possible to use a format similar to the "national drivers test" for this show. Indeed, this format might have relevance to a number of the shows I am suggesting for your consideration.

Styles of Education

There is considerable concern today about the educational system. A number of "objective" indicators suggest that there has been a precipitous decline in the ability of schools to educate according to industrial-era norms. Other indicators show serious breakdowns in discipline in the schools, assaults on teachers, high levels of vandalism. It is increasingly agreed that something is going seriously wrong and that changes must be made. As in so many other areas, however, there is no consensus about what should be done.

Finding new possibilities is very urgent because there is clear evidence of a type of "battle fatigue" among teachers. The best teachers are leaving because they do not feel that they are achieving their goals.

queries
and
comments

(It would be important in this show to remind people that although declining numbers are a critical problem in many parts of the United States the education system does not face a decline in numbers everywhere. There are geographical areas in the South which are still growing and therefore requiring new school buildings. Because of the general acceptance of the idea that managing decline is today's critical issue, these school and college districts are finding it increasingly difficult to get attention from their peers and from the institutions which should be helping them.)

As is natural, schools confronted with this pattern of breakdown are reacting with an attempt to return to the last period when they appeared to be successful. This leads to the "back to the basics" approach which has gathered so much support, at least on the surface. Such a move might, of course, be effective if conditions were the same as they were when the schools were last successful. Unfortunately, changes have been so great that new directions are obviously necessary.

But it might be possible to meld some of the needed new ideas with the pressures which lie behind the "back to the basics" movement. There is truth in the complaint that we have developed more fringes around education than we can well afford. Education, along with all other parts of the society, is going to have to give up some of the luxuries which it gained in the expansive period of the sixties and learn to work more effectively with more limited resources. (The challenge is not confined to education, of course, for it seems only too probable that we have built more capital stock throughout the society than we can afford to keep up given the increasing cost of both energy and materials.)

Maybe the key question for the show should be: "What are the twenty-first-century basics?"

We could ask different groups in the society to set out their ideas about what educational efforts are absolutely necessary, and we could again ask viewers to vote on what they saw. We could approach the Daughters of the American Revolution, the American Education Association, a couple of classrooms of kids, teachers being trained at a teachers' college, an effective parent–teacher association. We could provide each of these groups with a wide range of tools for presentation of their ideas through improvisational theatre, computer graphics, videotape presentations, etc.

queries
and
comments

We could also talk to a number of people who are working at the frontiers of their disciplines. We could ask them what a child, born this year, should learn in order to live well in the twenty-first century. What types of skills will be required? Where will the opportunities and the challenges be? Is our present educational style a hangover from the industrial era as some people claim? What would a communications-era educational style look like?

Levels of Morale

There have been substantial declines in the level of morale in America and indeed in almost all the rich countries of the world. This show would start with the evidence of this trend, probably presented in graphic terms.

After laying the groundwork, the show would look primarily at two sets of issues. First, what are the causes of the decline in morale? We would explain the various ways in which different types of thinkers have seen the problem.

1. There are those who believe that we have been going through a temporary time of troubles and that the morale problems which have resulted from these patterns will decrease as we move out of the current difficult period. In other words, one recipe for the future is to sit tight and to wait until the problems go away.

2. A second model would suggest that the problems have arisen because we have lost our nerve and have ceased to strive. We have not made the necessary effort to struggle for the available increase in the standard of living. Those holding this view argue that we shall not resolve the morale problem until we get back on a growth track for the socio-economy.

3. Still others would suggest that morale problems reflect fundamental realities. It is argued that we are moving inexorably toward a collapse and that the people who are worried see the inevitability of the collapse without knowing what to do about it. Those holding this view claim that one should do as much as one personally can to prepare for the crash but that it is too late to do anything at the social level to prevent it.

4. Another group argues that the frustrations of the present time are arising because governments at all levels are unable to see the profound changes in directions which are necessary. Government should be moving us as rapidly as possible out of the high-technology and high-growth patterns of

the past and into a situation where we can "live lightly" and in accordance with ecological realities. From this point of view, morale problems result from the recognition by the public of the need for fundamental change and the failure of the government to be supportive of the required changes.

5. The final group that we would deal with in this show argues that the central problem emerges from the confusion which exists at the present time. It claims that people are so confused that they no longer have any sense of how they can be effective either in their private or their community lives. This causes people to withdraw into privatism. This in turn leads to a sense of frustration and bafflement. One possible end result would be a search for a dictator.

The voting pattern in this program would have to be set up in such a way that people could demonstrate, if they wished, that they supported more than one of the views listed above. This procedure would take account of the reality that people have different visions of appropriate futures when they are with different groups. This multiple schizophrenia is highly destructive at the present time. Thought about varying visions, on the other hand, might lead to creative new ideas.

Acceptability of High Technology

Until the mid-sixties there were few doubts in the United States about science and technology. Growth was good and science and technology were the way to achieve it. Today the situation is far more mixed. There is evidence of a significant Neo-Luddite movement which aims to stop or slow the spread of modern technology. (This group is named after Ludd who smashed machines in Britain in the first half of the nineteenth century.)

It is often quite difficult to remember how much attitudes have changed in the last fifteen years. At the beginning of the sixties, murals at the Du Pont Company depicted smokestacks throwing out clouds of smoke—this was seen as a sign of prosperity. By the beginning of the seventies, these murals were perceived as evidence that Du Pont was not ecologically conscious: they had to be changed.

What had happened? We began to understand that the secondary and tertiary consequences of science and technology were not necessarily favorable. Technology assessment and environmental impact statements were introduced to provide a better measure of the implications which might follow from the introduction of new ways to doing things. Unfortunately, it now appears that the capacity of these techniques to provide unambiguous answers to highly complex questions is far more limited than had originally been hoped.

A number of people have therefore started to talk about "appropriate technology." Indeed, there are today a number of different movements which all use the term "appropriate technology" but mean very different things by it.

For most people "appropriate technology" means far lower levels of technology than have developed in recent years. It is argued that the present levels of technology are both too complex and too centralized. It is proposed that we should find ways to live more simply and to decentralize decision making as much as possible.

This group is confronted by another group which argues that the only hope for the future is the development of all the available technologies. Much of the argument on the nuclear question is at this philosophical level.

The potential synthesis of this argument lies in a *true* understanding of the term "appropriate technology." We need to ask what is appropriate for what purposes at what times. Those who hope for this type of discussion no longer accept that science and technology are automatically good or that they are automatically bad. This group is seeking for new conceptual tools which might permit society to make motivated decisions about the choices which lie before us.

The way into this show might be to remind people of what the automobile was thought to imply for the society and then to show what developments were in fact created: in other words, to contrast the expected and unexpected benefits and dangers which resulted from the car's spread throughout the total society. One might then demonstrate some other possible technologies which could spread throughout the society in the same way and ask people to consider some of the possible secondary and tertiary consequences of such developments. One could also ask people when they expected certain developments to take place given varying sets of priorities in the society. Obvious candidates for these questions would be telecommunications, biological interventions, and space exploration.

The Politics of Economics

It is the primary task of economics to maintain full employment.

This belief is the sacred cow which has grown up in the last thirty-five years. Even in those countries where unemployment is being created by government policies, it is argued that unemployment is a temporary situation which is necessary for the moment but which will be reversed as soon as possible.

No intelligent discussion of economic policy is possible until we reconsider this sacred cow. The barriers to even raising such an issue are almost insuperable, but the task must be begun.

Demand and supply-side economists agree on the need for low unemployment and maximum growth. No help is available from either side of the current cliché debate about economic policy: if we are to see clearly we must move further afield.

For many years now, there has been a constant call for a new Keynes, an economist who would put the pieces back together again as Keynes did through his work in the 1930s. Keynes revived economic growth by stressing the importance of consumption as compared to production.

The revolution in the culture and the breakdown in societal patterns which followed from this approach are only now being appreciated. The constant striving to meet impossible personal standards has given rise to jealousy among the "haves" and increasing anger among the "have-nots."

The new Keynes we have been looking for should, according to the conventional wisdom, find ways to meet the economic problems created by the old Keynes. He should cut through the Gordian knot which has been created by the linking of inflation and unemployment: low unemployment leads to high inflation and high unemployment is considered necessary to cut back on inflation.

The difficulty with this prescription is that the causes of our problems today are not economic but social. The role of economics in finding cures must be subsidiary to the rebuilding of effective neighborhoods and communities and the reintroduction of values which will reinforce rather than destroy social solidarity.

The critical change in positive terms will be a recognition of the need for profound alterations in life styles and life cycles to face new realities. Resource and energy limitations, the impact of computers and robots, and demands for new international economic systems to ensure greater justice will all require that we recognize the infeasibility of striving for maximum growth and maximum employment.

We have forgotten that these goals of maximum growth and maximum employment were originally seen as means to an end— the provision of opportunities for responsible individuals and continuing support for a functioning social system.

For several decades, we have enabled economists to set the terms of the overall national debate about directions. So long as we do this, we shall fail to come to grips with the urgent issues of the eighties. The 1981 riots and looting in Britain show the consequences of narrow economic policies which ignore social realities.

Present policies in America will kill hope as surely as they have in Britain. To move beyond this danger, we must demand that economists turn their skills to analyzing how to meet social goals rather than determining the evolution of cultural norms on the basis of their fixation toward the goals of maximum employment and maximum growth.

Law vs. Mediation/Arbitration

We have become an extraordinarily litigious society. The costs of this situation are greatly increased by the fact that legal processes rarely lead to conclusions satisfactory for all those involved. The law, with relatively rare exceptions, creates win/lose situations rather than win/win patterns.

Our continuing drift into the courts seems to reflect, at least in part, our deep pessimism about the behavior patterns of other human beings. For example, if it is suggested that a no-fault, no-lawyer divorce pattern might improve human relationships, one is reminded of the horror stories which developed because all contingencies were not legally specified.

Another difficulty with developing legal patterns is that one can be sued for practically anything at practically any time. More and more people are therefore steering clear of situations in which they might be exposed to legal liability even though their failure to become involved may reduce the possibility of effective initiatives taking place. All of us know of activities which would have been tried if people and institutions had not been advised that the activity might put them at risk. Today, for example, all major—even minor —corporate activities are cleared by lawyers.

There is a fundamental issue behind much of this legal activity. Let us take, for example, the problem of medical malpractice. (Legal and educational malpractice suits are also developing.) It is no defense to argue that one did one's best with what was available at the time. Even less is it a defense to argue that one made an honest mistake.

But we now know that striving for zero-risk situations is infeasible at best and dangerous at worst. It follows then that suing people for mistakes or misjudgments will necessarily gradually reduce the willingness to take chances. This will be surely disastrous in a society which needs change.

We could start this show with some "Perry Mason" dramas

which are based on the assumption that Perry is able to pull a miracle out of the hat during every show. Then we could go on to show the less glamorous and frustrating side of the law which the average citizen never really perceives unless he or she becomes involved. We could point out the number of cases in which the differences were not really "legal" but rather resulted from people living close to each other and trying to use limited space in conflicting ways where compromise was required.

We could then introduce people to the concept of arbitration and mediation and the effort made by people using these techniques to try to find "space" where everybody can gain from agreement. We might even be able to set up a case in which the viewer would be able to "arbitrate" a mock case: the results in the arbitration could be part of the feedback process on the show.

queries
and
comments

Decision Making

People are beginning to question the types of planning which have been used in the past. These have often assumed that it is possible to determine exactly how all the steps in a process could be put together, to anticipate all the events which could take place, to make the "best" set of decisions.

There have now been enough failures using these types of planning processes that real, fundamental questions are being asked about the viability of the models that are being employed. For example, we act as though it is possible to plan national and world economies but every year the directions which emerge are very different from those planned. We also act as though it is possible to determine how land use should be planned, but unforeseen events continue to destroy the careful directions that have been set.

This program would try to determine whether the failures in planning emerge from the fact that people are not bright enough to use available tools well or whether the tools themselves are inappropriate for use in a complex, interconnected society. It will be suggested that "planning," as it is presently understood, is an industrial-era technique which is inappropriate in today's conditions.

It would be fun to show on the home screen the planning games which have been used to teach people the strengths and weaknesses of the planning process. We could demonstrate that very different perceptions of self-interest which are inevitable between individuals and institutions must make events uncertain. Indeed, this is merely an enlargement of Heisenberg's famous uncertainty principle which shows that merely observing an event will alter it.

71

Obviously, actions of people who see their self-interest affected by planners will have an even more powerful influence on events.

One response to this set of criticisms about the "planning" process has been to develop a new rhetoric which suggests the desirability of an extreme form of "participatory democracy." But just as it is impossible for experts to plan *for* the people in acceptable ways, it is equally impossible for people to know enough about technical issues to make good choices *without help.*

We need to look for a synthesis between these two extreme views. A great deal of the theoretical work now being developed in various subject areas deals with this issue. The challenge will be to present the available material in ways that catch the attention of the viewer.

We may, however, have the necessary "hook." All too many people are now well aware that there is a failure of decision making throughout the society. A show that promises to illuminate this issue and to suggest even the beginnings of ways to break out of this problem might well get the attention of people at various levels of the society. The management issue is as confusing and frustrating in a small town in Iowa as it is in the Congress of the United States.

Are There Limits to Equality?

One of the main drives of federal policy in the seventies has been to equalize conditions as much as possible. Thus, there is a requirement that women athletes in college should have equal possibilities with males, that handicapped people have equal access to education, etc.

It is easy to show that such a policy can have absurd results when applied in real conditions. There has been pressure, for example, to permit wheelchair athletes to compete with runners in minimarathons: there have been times when the wheelchair "runner" has won.

On a different level, the requirement that all educational establishments be open to handicapped people of all types has placed, and is placing, enormous cost burdens on educational institutions at a time when their financial situation is increasingly difficult because of the dual impacts of inflation and the decreasing population using educational facilities.

Could this type of policy be further extended? There have been arguments that recreation facilities should not be restricted to those who are hale and hearty; some of the opposition to wilderness areas comes from the fear that older, sicker people will be excluded.

On the other hand, more and more people are arguing that the costs of "equality education and legislation" may well exceed the benefits. For example, it is not clear that the blind child, integrated into a classroom with sighted people, will do as well as a child in a classroom with other blind students: always assuming that we are prepared as a society to make sure that the needs of blind and other handicapped students are treated appropriately. It is our unwillingness to commit ourselves fully to the diverse needs of various populations which drives us toward an extreme "equality" model in the United States.

We must face hard choices which are based on difficult philosophical arguments. Some of the issues that we need to consider are:

queries and comments

Is there a right to risk and to fail? Does the attempt to make *everybody* "succeed" have a damaging effect on those individuals who would normally lead the society?

How much of a safety net can one build to protect the failures of the society without both encouraging further failure and preventing the success of those who are willing to strive?

Can the damaging effects of societal safety nets be changed by altering the process of education and socialization which goes on in societies? What sort of approach is needed in the United States to deal with our present conditions?

How can we make up for the effects of past injustice without causing new patterns of injustice? The inability of the Supreme Court to resolve this issue in the Bakke case shows the dangers that may develop in this area, particularly as the white, middle-class male sees his chances limited by the attempt to promote women and minorities. The post–World War II baby boom will also have significant impacts.

It is clearer and clearer from system theory that diversity—the acceptance of different life styles and patterns of behavior—is a requirement for a functioning system. Just as an ecological system requires a diversity of organisms if it is to survive stress, so a society requires a variety of different ways of seeing the world if it is to be able to manage the process of adaption to change.

Indeed, there are some social thinkers who argue that one of the greatest threats at the present time is that there is too little variation in the perceptions of those making decisions about the future of the United States and the world and too little under-

queries
and
comments

standing that real differences in views are reasonable. The challenge of this subject will be to create ways to visualize these issues on the screen.

Your Reactions

How would you respond to this letter and its appendix, acting in your assumed role?

Is the idea feasible from your point of view? Is it one you *should* work for? Is it one that you can pull off? What proposals would you make for changes in the ideas? What are the snags? Would you opt for different subjects? Would you want different emphases?

Now, returning to your own activities, how could the groups with which you are associated in real life support such a program if it were set up? How could you help? What difficulties might you have convincing people that this programing is a good idea—assuming you think that it is? At what levels of the organizations to which you belong would you encounter most difficulty, and where would you meet the most enthusiasm?

The final part of this book tries to help you to look in new ways at the questions in the preceding paragraphs.

5 Understanding and Acting in Today's World

In Chapter 2 I began by setting out four scenarios. By now you will have recognized that I believe that the overwhelming weight of evidence demands that we move toward an understanding of the management/transformational model.

The term *transformational* is used by various groups who all believe that we are entering a new era which will be as different from the industrial era as the industrial era was different from the agricultural.

In making this statement, people do not assume that industry will vanish in this new period any more than agriculture vanished in the industrial era. They are arguing that the dominant dynamics of this new era will be quite different from those which have existed in the past.

People have therefore chosen many different labels to describe this new era. I call it *the communications era* not only because communications is replacing transportation as the dominant technology but also because there is an absolute necessity for more effective communication between individuals and groups than there has been in the past.

This requirement for more effective communication stems from the pace of change which has been documented throughout this book. For the first time in human history, survival requires the development of a *totally* new set of understandings. This can only be achieved by effective, creative, and imaginative communication between those who see different parts of the changing realities.

But this in turn forces profoundly new educational models as compared to those which efficiently supported industrial-era patterns and styles of behavior. I discussed these realities before the Subcommittee on Elementary, Secondary and Vocational Education of the House of Representatives in the spring of 1979.

Creating a Desirable Educational System

The fundamental educational issues today are:

1. Is the educational system functioning so badly and are the present directions so unsatisfactory that fundamental change is required?

75

2. If the answer to the first question is yes, as I believe it to be, what are the feasible and desirable changes?
3. Of equal importance, what are the ways in which information about these feasible and desirable changes can be made available to those directly involved with education as well as to the American people in general?

Having made my position clear from the very start, let me enlarge upon our current problems and possibilities in the remarks that follow. First, we must recognize that in order to discuss education effectively we must share some understandings of the basic underlying purpose of education. Let me suggest to you that education, in its broadest sense, should act to prepare people to be successful in the world which will exist during their life span.

The educational system we now possess was designed to prepare people to live in the industrial era. What did the industrial era require? It needed a well-disciplined factory and office labor force who would stay on the job, obey orders, and be as efficient as possible. Society needed people who believed that hierarchical systems were the ways to get things done: orders were therefore obeyed without question. We also developed a situation in which people would always have unsatisfied desires for goods and services so that they would not continuously quit their jobs as they gained "enough" money as was the pattern in the nineteenth century.

In order to minimize misunderstanding, let me make it clear that I am not arguing whether the directions of the industrial era were good or bad. I am stating that childrens' attitudes in the late twentieth century are obviously very different from those which developed in the nineteenth. The question we must examine is whether this industrial-era set of attitudes is appropriate to the new set of conditions that are now developing in the United States.

Before going on to this subject we must recognize that, as might be expected, the school was organized to function along the same lines as the rest of the industrial-era system. The teacher was the equivalent of the "boss" in the office and the factory: the teacher both knew what needed to be known and was responsible for maintaining order. Thus the student, during his school years, not only learned the basics which were essential for efficient work in the industrial era but also absorbed the styles of behavior which would stand him or her in good stead as he or she entered the labor force.

What then was the basic epistemology which lay behind industrial-era thinking? It was believed that the universe worked according to comprehensible and learnable laws. A favorite image in the

nineteenth century was that of a clock wound up by God: human
beings might eventually learn to some extent to understand the way
in which the clock worked, but they would never be wise enough to
tamper with its operations.

Given the belief that people were unable to learn enough to
understand the universe, the obvious step to deal with the excessive
complexity of the universe was to divide knowledge into smaller and
smaller parts. Thus, we started with the major disciplines such as
physics, chemistry, economics, law, medicine, etc. Then we split into
subdisciplines and sub-subdisciplines until the specialist in one are
was totally unable to understand another specialist, even in the same
area of knowledge. This process of fragmentation still continues and
is now widely held to be the cause of many of our problems.

As a response to this situation, it is now generally agreed that
we should reintegrate knowledge into more usable forms. But efforts
toward this goal have all too often been unsuccessful. "Interdisciplinary" has seldom meant a well-understood body of knowledge
which can be taught in fundamentally new ways—rather it has
meant that specialists in different areas continue to state their limited
visions within the confines of a single course.

The hard fact is that we have entered a different world based
on a fundamentally different philosophy and epistemology. This
inevitably requires both the teaching of new bodies of knowledge and
also the teaching of these different bodies of knowledge in new ways.
Instead of the belief that the world is a clock wound up by God, we
now see the world as an extraordinarily complex organism in which
the actions of any part of the organism affect the behavior of other
parts of the organism, and in some cases the total organism.

This overall pattern of understanding has not yet been incorporated into our decision-making patterns nor into the educational
process which we use to inform people about the society. It may
therefore be important to look at the three strands which form this
overall pattern:

—First, the understanding that everything is connected to everything else. One can neither effectively study a subject nor act creatively without recognizing that all actions have consequences, and
that these consequences continue to reverberate through the socioeconomic system for indefinite periods of time. All too often the
secondary and tertiary effects of decision making may contradict and
annul the first intentions. Or to put it another way, there are very
few points at which a decision will really change the direction of a
society—many action patterns fail to be effective over time because

queries
and
comments

77

the desired change cannot be achieved in the particular way that is tried.

—Second, there is no such thing as objective analysis or action. We are all biased. Our biases emerge from our experience, and different people will see the same situation differently. It is hopeless to strive toward an absolutely "correct" answer, for nobody is going to be willing to admit that their "truth" is wrong. It may, however, be possible to approach the truth on a gradual basis as people listen to others and learn new perceptions and ideas which they had previously ignored or not perceived at all.

—Third, all action is risky. There are no certainties in life. One must always balance probabilities. Thus there is no absolutely "right" or "wrong" set of actions. In addition, people with different personalities and styles of thinking will want to accept different levels of risk and challenge.

If the world is interconnected, if objectivity is impossible, and if risk is inevitable, we clearly need to teach people new patterns of thought, and we need to teach them these new patterns of thought in new ways. This is the fundamental challenge which confronts education at all levels. It is not enough to make small modifications within current patterns. It is the *overall patterns themselves* which are making it impossible for us to provide children, and indeed adults, with the conceptual skills they need to deal with the patterns of events which surround them in today's world.

Thus, for example, we find the complexity of events continuing to increase. Most people find themselves hopelessly confused by the pace and pattern of events in the world today. They will continue to be unable to make sense of their world as long as they try to analyze it within the industrial-era models which they have been taught—models which require that events be predictable, understandable, and one-dimensional. We have to learn to operate with a far greater tolerance of ambiguity than has ever been the case in the past.

In addition, all of us must be aware of certain driving forces which seem likely to change the world in which we all live. By "driving forces" I mean critical factors which are affecting our universe and are not likely to be significantly affected by policy decisions over the next two decades.

What then are the primary skills we need to teach if we are to be able to live in the society that we have ourselves created in past years?

Let me suggest the following five needs. I do not believe that these can be listed in order of importance for they are *all* required if we are to be able to prepare people to live successfully in what I choose to call the communications era.

1. We must help people to gain the skills which will enable them to live happily and creatively with others in their communities. We must recognize that for this to be possible we shall need to create a far greater diversity of communities than presently exists in America and make it easier for people, as they grow and change, to move from community to community so that their skills can be more effectively used.
2. We must help people to be aware of their strengths and their weaknesses and provide them with the information and knowledge that will enable them to chart a life course which will be satisfactory to them and supportive of the communities in which they choose to live. It is in this context that the idea of learning to learn—rather than learning a subject once and for all—is critical.
3. We must teach people the ability to look at a defined situation and to make good decisions about the best ways to deal with that situation. This ability would foster an awareness of the interconnection of all life and understanding of the patterns of risk involved in any decision making.
4. We must teach people the ability to look at a situation and to come up with imaginative and creative ideas about the ways in which that situation can be changed for the better, so that all those involved in it have more chances of meeting their purposes and their goals.
5. We must teach people the ability to distinguish between situations in which it is wise to work within current realities and those that can only be resolved on the basis of creative thinking and significant change.

What implications do these suggestions have for present patterns of education? Many of the following ideas have been around for many years, but they have not affected significantly the momentum of the educational establishment. It is my hope that the meaning of these ideas will emerge far more clearly in the broader context sketched above.

1. Education must be lifelong: people must have the chance to continue to learn as long as they are alive. In a risky, uncertain, interconnected world one can only survive if one continues to learn.

This goal is a common one and we have, of course, made some progress toward it. But we have not understood its full implications for primary, secondary, and vocational education. The relatively rigid age grading that exists in the schools does not recognize the reality that each person may need to learn different subjects at different ages.

The sooner we enable people of very different ages to learn together, the sooner we shall be able to begin to diminish some of the pathologies which have emerged from confining young people largely to talking to people in their own age group. Why are we unwilling to mix young, middle-aged, and old people in the same learning situation? The answers are to be found in our vision of education as a carefully orchestrated progression of learning which makes a child ready for the world of work and able to stay in it for the rest of his or her life. This model is not suitable for the world that I have described.

2. Education must cease to be largely confined to the school-room. It must emerge from it and be integrated with life.

Marshall McLuhan made this point a number of years ago. He tells of two kindergarten kids walking down the street and identifying the planes as they flew overhead. When they come to the school-room door, one of them turns to the other and says: "Let's go in and string those darn beads." I believe that we all need to ask ourselves how much of the present educational system consists in stringing "darn beads."

We have come to a point in which most schools are "reality poor" as compared to the outside environment and television. People all too often endure school because they must. In the central cities, schools are frequently the highest crime areas, and sending our children to them is equivalent to indoctrinating them into a criminal life style.

The present school system really grew like Topsy. We never have considered in depth the implications of the present situation in which people are educated primarily within classrooms for as many as twenty years. We need to rethink how much of a person's educational life should be spent in a classroom and how much should be spent in dealing with real-life situations.

3. We need to recognize that, apart from a relatively limited core set of needs, different people need to be able to benefit from different educational experiences if they are to be able

to develop their strengths and minimize their weaknesses. The fundamental problem with much competency-based education today is that it tends to assume that *all* skills need to be achieved by *all* students. The result of this situation may be to force children to learn subjects in which they may *never* be competent rather than permitting them to develop their understandings and skills in those areas where they might become exceptional thinkers.

queries
and
comments

There is an assumption, built deep into our educational system, that the average student wants to do as little work as he or she can. If this is true, it follows that the only way that the educational system can be successful is to force learning on students. There is considerable evidence that this viewpoint is incorrect. First, we know that students who are effectively challenged by teachers tend to do very well in their studies. Second, there is evidence that students who are given a chance to state their needs are very often highly aware of them.

The psychology of the present educational system has deep roots in the puritan ethic. We have not rethought it in the light of our new learnings which show that people are capable of rising to challenges when they are given an opportunity to do so.

4. There is a need for more effective community control of the educational system. We use this rhetoric frequently, but the harsh reality is that the average local schoolboard does not have enough up-to-date information to be able to make good decisions.

If the rhetoric about local control is to become real, we must take two steps. First, we must improve the access of the interested local schoolboard to imaginative and creative thinkers in the field of education. Second, we must find ways in which people in the community can more effectively communicate their feelings about appropriate styles of education to the teaching and administrative staff of the local educational bodies.

The primary result of this type of education would be to improve our ability to manage our own lives and to make decisions about the communities in which we live, the systems of which we are a part, and the cultures which mold our lives.

Although such a goal is difficult to achieve, it is not unrealistic. A program which started at Eastfield College in the Dallas Community College District in May 1980 demonstrates that such a goal can be reached.

queries
and
comments

Involving Educators

The program started on the basis of two critical assumptions. First, people are not apathetic. Rather, they are baffled and frustrated by a world in which the patterns of behavior they learned in the past no longer provide desirable results. This assumption was tested again and again and proved to be valid.

Second, any attempt to move an organization or a community as a whole is doomed to failure. The only hope is to work with those who are ready to take risks toward what they see as desirable change. Unfortunately, models which take this stance are often rejected as elitist by those who argue that these models fail to give everybody an equal, initial chance. The fact that a dynamic may be established in this way—as was the case at Eastfield—which will eventually give everybody new opportunities is ignored.

The specific program described here emerged from the fact that morale at Eastfield had dropped precipitately over the past year. A basic theme of improving the quality of life was therefore adopted. It was stressed from the beginning of the program that various driving forces were now impinging on the culture so strongly that people would be forced to change their behavior if they wanted to meet their goals in the late twentieth and early twenty-first centuries. The driving forces studied were those listed in Part III of this book.

At the beginning of the 1980/81 school year, the president of the college, Eleanor Ott, used the normal opening activities for faculty, administration, and staff to introduce the idea of change through the driving forces. Small groups were then set up to make suggestions for ways in which the quality of education and life at the college could be improved.

The fear was that these groups would turn into gripe sessions. But due partly to the careful development of facilitating skills and also to the fact that people tend to rise to real challenges, a large number of intelligent suggestions were made which were then widely circulated.

This initial effort sparked the interest of a significant number of people in the continuing development of the program. The first step was to convince those involved that there was no fixed program or hidden agenda—that we were looking for all the activity and imagination we could obtain.

The next step was to create a *situational*—a shared set of jokes and myths—which would hold the group together. This emerged quite unexpectedly in the "pink ladies" who spoofed the feminine styles of previous generations. This pattern, which started as a one-time event, became the glue that carried the college past many difficult moments. We all too often forget that effective social action depends on emotional and social glue as much as on rational social purposes: inability to understand this reality will inevitably lead to failure.

By the end of the year a core group of some twenty to thirty people—faculty, staff, administration, and students—were jointly planning a continuation of the program for the next year. Month-long programs on four of the driving forces were being planned: outside speakers were being recruited and, even more importantly, faculty were modifying classes to teach within this overall framework.

More surprisingly, other college groups which had never been directly involved with the quality of life effort were setting up converging programs. For example, a large faculty group got together to examine the "quality of education" at a retreat at the very end of the academic year when energy usually slumps. Indeed, by the end of the year there was a tendency to call any novel activity that did not fit within the normal organizational patterns a "quality of life" effort. We were continuously surprised by the "quality of life" activites of which we had never heard until they surfaced.

There was general agreement by the end of the academic year that significant institutional renewal had taken place. From my point of view, four factors had been critical, Some of them have already been mentioned but they need to be stressed:

1. The president of the college, Eleanor Ott, was highly supportive.
2. There was a tradition of excellence.
3. The program was coordinated by a remarkable individual, Kathryn Berry, who understood that maintenance of human relations was more critical than formal authority lines.
4. The college was enabled/forced to look outward at reality by the discussion of the driving forces and by the continuing visits of an ousider—in this case myself. I was on campus about six times during the year.

The overall result was that a number of people were better informed as to the forces that would shape *their lives.* They were more able to think through the individual choices that they should make.

None of us involved would claim that people had become fully aware of the *specifics* of domestic and international policy. Indeed, I believe that striving for such a goal is unrealistic. J. Edward Murray, publisher of the *Boulder Daily Camera,* has long been aware of this reality. He claims that the newspaper in its present form is the enemy of democracy as is radio and television news. How, he asks, can the citizen be expected to believe in the importance of small, tedious steps toward more human and humane local systems when he is confronted daily by evidence of national and international breakdown?

On the other hand, people can and must be provided with enough information to make intelligent decisions about their own lives and their communities. This requires that each person be provided with the ability to:

1. understand his or her own character so that a life course can be created which will use the individual's skills and avoid his weaknesses;
2. understand the driving forces which will change societal and cultural realities in coming years and decades;
3. understand the ways in which actions cause feedback at the personal, economic, ecological, and cultural level so that actions do not lead to undesired second-and third-level consequences;
4. understand the basic physical science laws so that people do not contravene them in ways which bring undesired results.

The educational pattern which will achieve this result will stress self-knowledge, communications skills, and basic understandings of reality. It does not yet exist anywhere, to my knowledge, at the present time. It can only emerge from a marriage—perhaps a shotgun marriage—of educational threads which have previously been seen as mutually incompatible.

Management of Complex Systems

Introduction

Most people are not concerned with the overall pattern of public affairs. Those who are will need far better tools for structuring information than have ever existed in the past because of the rapid change. We must discover how to manage change effectively.

We must move far beyond the current cliché debates which examine dichotomized issues around the poles of low growth and high growth or simple technology as compared to complex technology. We must create an essentially new debate which covers fundamentally different issues.

President Reagan, President Mitterand, and Prime Minister Thatcher have all returned in their own unique ways to the platitudes of an earlier era. Our survival, let alone our ability to develop ourselves, depends on breaking out of current patterns of thought and understanding.

queries
and
comments

1. A Critique of the Extrapolist View

Each of us tends to look at the world as though our own view of it is correct. Today, we are all having increasing problems as we come to understand that different people have profoundly different visions of reality and that there is no "objective" way of sorting out which of these visions is correct. As a result we are beginning to understand the full implications of John Maynard Keynes's statement that "Practical men are all slaves of some defunct scribbler."

None of us can cope with *all* the realities of the world; they would overwhelm us. Each of us must develop organizing principles (or theories) which permit us to make sense of our own world. The need for change is being felt today because more and more of us sense that the ways to organizing reality we were taught by the culture do not work effectively for us.

Where do our management concepts come from? I think many of us will be surprised to discover that they are directly descended from the idea that God created the world, understood where it was going and that the things which happened in it were therefore desired and wished by him. Authority and power were therefore vested in a being who was inherently beyond our understanding, and it followed that we should be content with whatever happened. (Not so incidentally we should remember that this belief in man's control by God was, in its extreme form, always heretical: the central religious struggle has always been to understand the interplay between an autonomous individual with "free will" and the "will of God.")

The belief in an all-knowing God served as a practical support for authoritarian decision making by the popes. They claimed (and indeed claim to be) the direct line to God, and they therefore have the right in certain circumstances to speak "ex cathedra" as the direct representative of God. (Not all statements of the pope have this quality, of course.) Thus popes were seen as inherently superior to kings who also gained their authority from God but not directly. Popes therefore wielded enormous authority because of this situation.

However, as both piety and superstition declined, it became both possible and desirable for kings to deny that the pope had a better line to God than they did. King Henry VIII gained increased authority by successfully challenging the power of the pope. He continued to maintain his own legitimacy, however, by stating that he still had his direct line to God—if by a different route.

The societal credibility of this claim continued to decline over the centuries, but the belief that individuals who held positions of power were inherently better able to make good decisions continued to exist. Until quite recently, we have invested prime ministers and presidents of countries with a quasi-mystical aura, believing that the office carried with it some assurance of almost superhuman wisdom.

Our belief in the extraordinary potential of those with power was centrally linked with our understanding of the operation of the world as mechanical. If, by chance, something went wrong the person at the top of the system was believed to be in the best position to find out what had gone wrong and to mobilize the resources required to mend it. This assumption was essentially logical, given the pattern of assumptions, because the power to learn what was going on and the power to act could "obviously" be best mobilized by the person at the top of the society.

This model of power and authority was seen as valid throughout the society until recently. Legitimacy was assumed for people at the top of all organizations, whether they got there through voting, or promotion through the ranks of a business or a church, etc. (However, we have, as a society, tended to challenge the ways that people in other societies use to reach the top of their societies and thus become able to exercise structural authority.)

It was only possible to maintain the "legitimacy" of this model of power and authority by stressing the machine-like nature of the society. The person holding structural authority was assumed to be confronted by relatively few problems needing decisions—"the government is best that governs least." It was usually assumed that the proper way to handle problems was to return to the status quo ante: to put the system back into its previous situation.

It is possible to track simply—but inevitably superficially—the process by which breakdown in the belief in this clockwork system model developed. Toward the end of the nineteenth century, the levels of social injustice and economic malfunction were so great that measures to change the system were demanded and passed. Each malfunction, however, was treated as a separate problem and a cure for each was created.

In the mid-thirties, there was a catastrophic collapse in the total system. At this point most people and the government that represented them agreed that fundamental change was needed. The right of the government to alter the socioeconomic system was conceded and a number of measures—such as Social Security were introduced: these had far greater impacts than their originators had expected.

queries
and
comments

It was in this climate that John Maynard Keynes introduced his "revolutionary" idea that governments could effectively control "trade cycles." This thinking was seen as naive and irresponsible originally, but its post-World War II successes were so dramatic that Keynes's ideas were rapidly adopted. Administrations began to present themselves as active changers of the Newtonian mechanism which was seen to deliver unsatisfactory results.

The high point of this interventionist model came in the Kennedy and Johnson years. The people that Kennedy recruited held a passionate, if simplistic, belief that the society could be changed to be more just and more humane. Legislation was proposed to deal with many of the traditional evils of the society. Heavy resistance was encountered from Congress and the country: they were far from certain that they wanted to adopt the highly interventionist model being pushed by Kennedy. It is a highly fascinating "what if" to wonder what would have happened if Kennedy had not been assassinated.

In reality, of course, the death of Kennedy opened up a flood of legislation. It was felt that we "owed" Kennedy what he would have wanted. A great many badly conceived laws were passed and the breakdown of many of them was inevitable from the start.

As policy failures proliferated, politicians wanted more and more information in a form which they could use. They were unwilling to tolerate presentations from a large variety of different viewpoints and they therefore tried to obtain an overall picture which would set out the type of policies which needed to be followed. The word interdisciplinary came into vogue both within university structures and outside them: more and more groups became involved in problem solving.

An extraordinary number of new structures developed; they were often called Institutes. Some of them were general in nature, prepared to take on practically any task, and they claimed wide competence. Others were concentrated in areas such as poverty or housing or rural development or health. However, reports from these structures were nearly always based on the assumption that there was a single right way to look at the issue being studied. It was also rather generally assumed that it was possible to develop a single, unambiguous set of policy recommendations to deal with the realities which had been described.

The failures of the sixties and seventies made us wary of this belief. We have discovered that the war on poverty didn't work. The effort to improve the educational system has largely failed. The sickness system has been consolidated rather than altered to encourage the promotion of health. There is more crime than ever before. The backlash against intervention led to the election of President Reagan, who clearly wishes to return to conditions which have already vanished.

When we recognize this reality we shall be led to new understandings. We will be forced to recognize that societies operate on organic rather than mechanical principles. We will learn that we cannot substantially change one element in a culture without changing all the culture.

It is increasingly obvious that we have a fundamentally malfunctioning system, and we are trying to deal with various failures through partial measures which cause further breakdowns elsewhere. This, in turn, creates additional immediate problems for those who are in decision-making systems—they then have even less time to think about how to achieve the fundamental changes which are required. It is not difficult to write a scenario based on current trends which would end in a profound breakdown in all of our systems.

The danger of this direction is greatly increased because we now "know" as a society that we cannot permit people to make decisions *just* because they hold power. The process of development of this feeling through many stages, including Nuremberg and Vietnam, is too lengthy to track here. The reality, however, is that we are trying to run a complex interrelated society on the basis of a set of assumptions which not only are known to be invalid intellectually but which the general public no longer believes.

2. The Issue Viewed From the Romantic Viewpoint

There have been many attempts during the industrial era to build more human and humane institutions. These attempts started from a desire to honor the dignity of the individual. Unfortunately, most planners of institutions that aimed toward a more human future failed to understand the constraints of the society or the forces which could undermine their hopes.

This pattern has been seen in a large number of cases throughout the nineteenth century. The Owenites, the Shakers, etc., shared a belief that they should reform the society by setting a better example. In almost all cases, their institutions died out or were changed so radically by outside pressures that they failed to fulfill the dreams of their founders.

Much the same pattern developed with the communes in the sixties: a large number of people hoped to set up alternative human patterns of living. Typically, these communes lasted a shorter time than the intentional communities of the nineteenth century. There would appear to have been two predominant reasons for this less permanent pattern: First, a great many of the people who entered the commune movement really did not have a clear idea of the type of society they wanted to create. Second, the degree of impermanence and lack of norms in the society affected the people in the commune movement as well as the rest of the society.

The romantics start from the correct assumption that institutions cannot be effective unless they are composed of decent people. Tragically, however, they often do not perceive that while this is a necessary condition it is not a sufficient one. Decent people have all too often made a mess of deciding on the perceptions and norms which will enable them to create good societies. The continued wreckage of the high hopes with which alternative institutions start shows that the skills required for effective functioning are all too often not known or applied.

The typical pattern in the sixties and seventies seems to have been to try to minimize rules. The problem has been that a large number of specific problems then necessarily emerge which are all treated on an ad hoc basis. The consequent jumble of rules is then continued into conditions for which it was not designed and where it may not be at all appropriate.

queries
and
comments

1. The Challenge Viewed From the Communications Era

Those who still accept the extrapolist Newtonian model assume that we do live in a clockwork universe: the trends in the society are then considered to be stronger than the effects of either individual or group action. Those who accept romantic models argue that if one changes one's life style and that of one's group, there will be an alteration not only in one's own community but also in the way of life of the overall society.

People who are trying to create the communications era are aware that the world is formed on the basis of self-fulfilling and self-denying prophecies. They know that people help to bring into existence the "realities" toward which they choose to strive and to prevent the emergence of those "realities" against which they exert their effort. There is no certain future: people determine what they obtain within broad limits. An old saying for children is "Be very careful what you want, you may get it." This is even truer for whole societies. It is in this context, also, that Winston Churchill's statement "We build our buildings and then our buildings build us" makes sense. (Modern physical sciences no longer know how to make a sharp distinction between reality and unreality; there are a number of possible states for a universe with different probabilities. The same theorizing applies for social systems: it is possible to change the probabilities of the existence/emergence of certain realities by the amount of effort that is made.)

This truth was well known to Joseph Schumpeter. He stated that there are very few things that are worth accomplishing that would be undertaken by a "rational" man. He was arguing that the truly worthwhile effort is one which changes the future toward a more desirable direction.

It follows that individual, group, and societal directions can be changed only if new concepts are understood. It is our collective inability to break out of our present way of seeing and organizing the world that is the real factor that prevents us from inventing the new society which we so urgently need. The "objective" studies we presently carry through do us great harm for they reinforce our belief that today's perceptions are accurate.

If an individual, group, or institution is to survive present traditional problems, three processes must be developed:

First, we must envisage our future in ways which excite us and allow us to break out of our present understandings. We must learn to look for and see relationships which are not obvious—or even visible—within the present type of world order.

Second, we must look back at our past and reexamine our personal, group, and societal histories. We now recognize that history is always written by the winners but we have still not dealt with the awkward reality that the winners may not inevitably have been right. The revisionist historians of the Civil War, for example, have raised some very awkward questions about the relative morality of slave ownership in the South and the patterns of job holding in the North.

Third, we must learn communication skills so that we can examine both past and future in the context of today and thus decide how the transformation is going to be effectively managed. We have been unable up to the present time to discover the ways in which we can help people to see how they can change their present ways of living and working without intolerably damaging their self-interest.

If we began to look at past, present, and future in these ways, what would we begin to see? We would discover that the concept of the universe as a clock has indeed been disproved by the work of such scientists as Einstein, Bohr, and Heisenberg. They have shown that everything does affect everything else, that realities are probabilistic and that uncertainty always exists in all situations. We are now confronted with the task of adapting these understandings to the social sciences and to management theory.

queries
and
comments

How can we do this? There is a danger that a recognition that everything affects everything else in probabilistic ways would paralyze us. We need to understand the world in which we live in order to be able to act, and we certainly cannot hope to understand everything in the world. We are therefore driven to accept that we shall always act on the basis of inadequate and incomplete knowledge and that the good decision maker will be the person who develops skill to cope with this reality. More and more studies are now being published which show the importance of "intuition" in management.

It is possible, however, to begin to develop ways of structuring knowledge which start from the reality that there is no objective truth, rather than from the Newtonian models which create a determination for each individual to state his own understanding and then to fight for it as the *only* truth. We need to look at each issue, to determine those factors which are most crucial, and to sort out the possible patterns of interconnections. We also need to recognize that the complexity of views is so great and the levels of uncertainty so high, particularly at this time, that we must prepare ourselves to meet an uncertain future.

Our present styles of high-powered competition—even deliberate conflict—add to the uncertainties that beset us. Because we must have a viable model of the world in which we live in order to make "reasonable" decisions, we cannot afford to make deliberate efforts to distort the truth in order to achieve narrow partisan advantage. It is my conviction that cooperation is therefore becoming a societal necessity. One reason that we do not accept this conclusion is that we assume that a cooperative universe would be a soft and flaccid one. On the contrary, trust relationships between people permit them to challenge each other's perceptions and beliefs in ways which are not feasible when people work together without knowing each other's concerns and passions.

One final, general theoretical point needs to be raised here. The evaluation of "failure" and "success" needs to be far more careful and complete than in the Newtonian universe. In a Newtonian universe, the meaning of success is relatively unambiguous. In a post-Newtonian era, we must recognize that each person and institution will define success differently and that evaluation of that individual or institution is not feasible until the defined success criteria are known. (It is fascinating that accrediting organizations in education increasingly demand that a school or college know what it wants, and that judging can only take place after these criteria are known.)

91

This is not the only difficulty in defining success and failure effectively. In many circumstances, it will be possible to come up with a fan of possibilities:

Route A leads to a small gain and has an 80 percent chance of success.

Route B leads to a medium gain and has a 50 percent chance of success.

Route C leads to a large gain and has a 20 percent chance of success.

If Route C is deliberately chosen, one cannot reasonably say that the choice was wrong because the route fails, for it was believed that the large chance of gain overpowered the fact that the odds were only 20 percent. It is also important to recognize that different temperaments will tend to choose different routes with different degrees of risk attached to them.

What then can we say about management in general terms?

1. Given the reality of diversity some people will be better in management roles than others. Similarly, some people will be better in high-risk situations than others. (We need to remember that these differences result from both genetic and specific educational/socialization processes. It is long past time to lay to rest the question of whether nature or nurture controls.)

A good management team is one in which people's temperaments fit the tasks they do and where an overall sense of purpose is created. However, despite talk of management approaches which are meant to stress both task accomplishment and personal satisfaction, we are still remarkably ineffective in permitting people to use their skills. For example, successful salesmen and teachers and engineers are often promoted to be administrators. Individuals accept the promotions in order to get more money even though task competence and work satisfaction may be decreased. It is this situation which leads to the reality and the pervasiveness of the Peter Principle.

2. It is obvious that the more closely a person observes a particular area, the more knowledgeable the person will become about it. Thus, bright salesclerks will have more knowledge about evolving sales trends in their own area than the executive who is responsible for their work. This factor has led to situations in which executives go out and work in the field so as to get an understanding of current realities; this trend is carried to its extreme in China. It has also caused an understanding of the need for more effective information transmission throughout companies.

The basic problem in promoting effective communication is the lack of trust—and even of a common language—between levels of a company. Messages do not necessarily reach the receiver in the form that is intended; this is particularly true when the sender is trying to get the receiver to pay attention to new trends. Changing the perceptions of people is difficult at the best of times; problems in this area are still further increased when information may well be threatening to the sender or the receiver or even both. It is important to recognize that there may be a threat from new information regardless of whether the information is moving up or down the company.

queries
and
comments

It is for this reason that "management by exception" remains more of a theory than a reality. It is relatively easy for subordinates to pass on information about problems that have already been defined as being of importance to the management of the company. It is extra ordinarily difficult for subordinates to find ways to inform their superiors of new trends; difficulties are compounded when a subordinate may only sense a shift in direction without being able to articulate it clearly.

Unfortunately, however, in today's world it is those things that we *don't know* that are likely to hurt us most seriously. Thus, the potential for an energy crisis was "obvious" to those who had analyzed the situation, but it was not taken into serious account even by most futurists, by most institutional decision-makers, and certainly not by the general public.

It seems clear to me that there are still many problems and possibilities which are relatively close, in terms of the time when they could happen, which we have not yet begun to integrate into our social planning:

—the fact that the energy shortage is only the leading edge of a raw materials crunch.
—concentration on the relatively controllable dangers of communist/capitalist strife rather than on North/South or rich/poor breakdown.
—exclusion of the dangers of chemical/biological warfare from discussion with all the stress on the danger of nuclear conflict.
—failure to perceive the impact of communication technologies over the next decade.

These examples taken at random could be increased several times.

The harsh fact is that we have not yet even developed, let alone adopted, communications and management techniques which would

93

enable people to perceive and grasp the new realities which surround us. I believe that there are two primary reasons for this. First, our underlying models assume that fundamental change does not and should not take place: this concept results from the Newtonian paradigm on which our social structures are based. Second, we are not yet aware of the extraordinary difficulty of getting people to accept new ways of looking at the world. We therefore continue to assume that the receiver obtains the message intended by the sender: it is only today that we are really coming to understand the extraordinary degree of distortion that can intervene between a sent and a received message.

The underlying implication of this argument is that we must change our understanding of patterns of authority. As we have seen, we have inherited a belief that position ensures wisdom and that the person holding a position of power has the information that he requires to behave wisely. We are now learning that this model is inadequate and that power can, in fact, distort information flows.

Lord Acton was aware of this when he stated: "Power tends to corrupt and absolute power corrupts absolutely." This statement has usually been treated as an aphorism. However, it becomes a sober factual reality when it is rephrased as follows: "Power tends to corrupt information and absolute power corrupts information absolutely." The statement then refers to the undeniable fact that people who are afraid of others will tend to give them inaccurate information and the greater the degree of power, the worse the information flows will tend to be.

What elements need to be taken into account as we try to manage the world socioeconomic system at the present time?

The following material is brief and tentative and will be enlarged as feedback comes in.

1. The trend in recent years and decades has been toward increased centralization of decision making and therefore increased power. This power therefore has led to increased distortion of information in an effort to ensure/force the most attractive decision for various groups: the pressure of different views on public and private decision making is increasingly unmanageable.

As I see it, our only present hope of gaining clarity is to bring together people to look at single problem/possibilities (issues) through widely divergent windows. They should then be challenged to define as clearly as they can the status of the general discussion of the subject. This information should then be made widely available to those who can benefit from it. This process of creating new knowledge is ideally carried through on a networking basis using people working in different interest areas.

2. The other challenge we face as a society is to carry through efficiently the tasks which *we have decided* are necessary rather than discussing what needs to be done. This requires well-organized systems which can act with maximum efficiency and minimum waste.

queries
and
comments

This type of action requires an organizational hierarchy, for the person at the top of the system should have the clearest overall perception of the nature of the task. Each person operating within the institution should then have the clearest possible perception of the task he or she is meant to perform and should be able to perceive if his/her way of performing his/her required activities is getting in the way of other necessary work. To do this, each individual must have a sense of the overall vision of the institution—this sense will be far clearer at the top, if the system is to work well, than at the bottom. However, in many types of activity, particularly service activities, the image of the institution will be made or broken in the lower ranks of the organization.

This set of statements leads to a different view of the nature of today's socioeconomic/political crisis than is usually advanced. In effect, one way of stating our current problem is that more and more issues are kept "permanently" open, and there is therefore no clear-cut, definable task before many institutions. For example, we are not prepared—once we have decided on the building of a power plant—to trust the utility company to build it to the best of its ability; there is thus widespread, continuing interference from many groups.

The essential reasons for this situation are clear. First, there are, as we have seen, *real* questions about appropriate directions, and people try to stop the development or continuation of a certain policy because they genuinely fear its consequences. Second, we have less and less faith in the honesty of systems, often including our own, and feel that somebody must look over everybody's shoulder to prevent bad behavior.

However, while the reasons for this situation are understandable, the consequences are disastrous. The waste of time and resources ensured by continuous changes in plans is increasingly intolerable in today's conditions. Effective societal management will require:

—agreed statements of the realities of our situation to be achieved by networking between individuals who belong to groups which normally have limited, or ineffective communication between them. This must be coupled with an understanding that utopias are not going to be achieved and that individuals, institutions, and societies will inevitably make mistakes.

—institutions with agreed missions must then act effectively to carry them out. (The word institution in this context means a structured set of activities; it should be carefully distinguished from an acceptance of bureaucracy. Bureaucracies are *one* type of institution.) While it is inevitable that mission statements will alter over time, we shall have to accept the reality that doing things is one primary way in which we learn, that having learned we could do what we have just done better but we cannot continuously revise our planning and preserve an acceptable degree of effectiveness.

Action and activity plans must be frozen at some point. If they are frozen too soon, they will incorporate too little of the available knowledge. If they are frozen too late or left permanently unfrozen, efficiency levels drop dramatically. To put it in a different way, action is necessary but if we do not know enough at the time the action is taken then many of the components of the activity may turn out to be unduly costly over the long haul.

We need to find ways to define the world in which we actually live and gain a general acceptance of this definition. We then need to act to meet the real needs of the situation. Both of these tasks will require levels of management which are far higher than those we are able to create at the present time.

Problem/Possibility Focusers

Introduction

The policy documents which are developed at the present time are naturally created to support industrial-era styles of management: they hide and even disguise the conflicts, disagreements, and trade-offs within the society. The object is either to develop clear-cut proposals which will be put into effect or, alternatively, to muddle the overall picture so completely that stasis is inevitable.

In a management/transformational world, the central need is to have available an overall picture of each relevant set of realities that exposes, rather than hides, the complexities and uncertainties but nevertheless makes clear the consequences of action and inaction. Such a framework of analysis requires a new form of document.

This document should set out as clearly as possible the existing agreements and disagreements so that these can be progressively refined. It may be assumed that many of the apparently irresolvable differences today do not emerge from real conflicts of interest but from different perceptions of reality—that individuals and groups which appear to disagree may be able to reach at least partial consensus if they will only listen to each other.

The technique described below has been tested out in a number of ways and under a number of conditions and has had useful results even though there has never been a full-scale test of the idea. More critically, a large number of documents are being created in similar forms as a result of parallel thinking and invention.

queries
and
comments

1. The Issue From the "Extrapolist" Viewpoint*

One of the most startling realities of the first half of the 1980s is the extent of the disagreement around today's critical issues. In the last decade the patterns of consensus which have made it possible to govern the United States and other Western societies have largely disintegrated. Various politicians today have radically different views about the nature of the problems which confront us, the values within which we should structure societies, the types of behavior which can be expected of human beings, and even the goals which can and should be achieved.

Our present political system is essentially based on an assumption that there will be a shared core of norms and beliefs which holds the society together: indeed, politics has been defined in the past as the process of eliminating the divergencies from this desired norm. There is necessarily a breakdown in policy making when the shared core of national beliefs fragments.

One can see this reality clearly by looking at the failure to develop an energy policy over recent years. Presidents have tried to convince Congress that there are self-evident realities within which policy should be made. It is now clear that many members of Congress, much of the public, and a large proportion of the special interest groups do not share the vision of presidents. Passage of any coherent energy policy is thus literally inconceivable.

Unfortunately, there is a built-in vicious circle which results from failure to keep up with changing circumstances. As people become more concerned about any area of policy, they become shriller in pushing for their alternatives. Those at the center of the decision-making process therefore find themselves undergoing ever more intense pressure: the facts, data, values, and theories which led to the policy suggestions of various groups are harder and harder to discern because they are buried under deeper and deeper piles of rhetoric. This in turn leads to power, rather than reality, having more and more impact on the decision-making process.

We are moving rapidly in this direction in all the most critical areas of our society. The pressures around the issues of employment,

---

*Extrapolist thinkers are those who do not anticipate much change in current patterns.

97

energy, food, ecology, housing, water, etc., are so intense that it is almost impossible for even the most concerned citizen or decision maker to sort out the realities. This is true also for any of the subissues within a field; for example, it is extremely difficult to understand what the real issues are in terms of the potential of solar, geothermal, and nuclear energy.

Many of those in the industrial-era, decision-making system are only too well aware of their situation, but they see no way to break out of it. The inertia and the survival instincts of all those within systems tend to reinforce their pathologies and to overwhelm the small and hesitant steps taken to change the dynamics which presently exist. Indeed, the central assumptions of the industrial-era system make it impossible to pay serious attention to communications-era concepts which emerge from a fundamentally different pattern of thinking.

There are two key assumptions in industrial-era decision making. First, it is believed that there is a right answer to any question and that this is known by the most expert individual or the most expert group. This approach results from the concept that it is possible to look at any situation objectively, to perceive all the realities within it, and for the person who is most skilled to give the right answer. It is this assumption which leads to the ever-growing conflict between "expert" testimony. Second, it is assumed that it is possible to consider the results of policies and actions in one field without thinking seriously about their interconnections with other areas of the socioeconomic system.

The committee structure which exists, for example, in the Congress and state legislatures is set up so that it is possible for people to consider energy policy without a systemic look at the consequences on ecology and the economy. It is seldom recognized that there are secondary and tertiary results of policies besides the desired primary effects. As people and systems become more sophisticated, they are learning to respond in ways which limit or palliate the negative effects of any particular act of legislation on them. This is the reason why most types of control measures, price control, for example, are necessarily ineffective.

It is fascinating that both positive and negative extrapolists (i.e., those who see the *certainty* of improvement *on* catastrophe) are willing to trust the same information-structuring techniques. While their conclusions about the future are diametrically opposed, the ways that they structure their thinking are very similar. To use a games analogy, those holding both viewpoints are willing to play baseball—although they differ about the way the game will come out.

2. The Issue From the Romantic Viewpoint.*

For the romantic, the ultimate reality is the individual's or the group's view of what exists and is happening. There has been little concern about the issues of societal governance, for the broad question of how to create societal consensus is either seen as automatically soluble by goodwill or ignored. Nevertheless, and paradoxically, the shift in thinking caused by the romantic vision can be the first step toward new patterns of understanding.

3. The Challenge Viewed From the Communications Era

Given these serious difficulties with our present decision-making system, why are people still so confident of our survival and success? The reason stems from another hidden assumption of the industrial era: our socioeconomic system is a machine which may break down but which can always be mended. Thus, it is assumed that although there will be sticky moments we shall eventually "muddle through."

But people who have learned system theory know that this is not an appropriate model. Cyclical behavior is apparently present in almost all systems, including complex natural systems, and we should therefore ask ourselves whether the patterns that exist at the present time in our society are healthy.

To do this we must recognize that systems behave in three ways: they have oscillations which decrease in magnitude, increase in magnitude, or are stable. (Systems are, of course, far more complex, but this statement is adequate for my purposes.) Think of a pendulum: if it swings the same distance each time it is a stable system; if it swings less and less each time it is a damping system; if it swings further and further each time it is an expanding system.

Systems which have increasing oscillations are unstable and will break down; the only question is when. Most system analysts would agree that the industrial era is suffering through cycles of increasing magnitude. It is for this reason that people who think in communications-era terms cannot accept that we will be able to continue to "muddle through."

Some examples may be useful. The First World War came about because the then-current world order was dramatically unstable. The shooting of a relatively minor figure (in an "unimportant"

*Romantics are people who believe that the primary issue is changing the ways that human beings behave.

part of the world) was sufficient to upset a system which appeared to most participants in it to be not only stable but also essentially eternal. Similarly, the Great Depression was triggered at a time when everybody "knew" that prosperity would continue forever. A growing number of people are afraid that the present national and international systems are equally unstable. The way in which the breakdown will develop will, of course, not be known until it happens.

One useful image is an avalanche. It is poised ready to descend from the shifting of one stone, the firing of a shot, a slight change in climatic conditions. It is not useful to search out the exact factor which caused the avalanche; rather, one must be aware of the quasi-certainty of the avalanche and act to minimize its effects either by avoidance if possible or by setting off the destructive energy in a way in which the consequences will be least damaging.

In effect, therefore, it is urgent that we recognize the instability of present systems and start to find ways to minimize the dangers which result from this instability. We also need to begin to create new information systems which defuse the instabilities which presently exist by helping people to gain different visions of their self-interest in the light of the new conditions which are emerging. We need to see that an effective community is one which can deal with its problems before they become acute and can recognize possibilities while they are available. The problem/possibility focuser is one technique designed to move us in this direction.

4. The Response

A. General Description

The problem/possibility focuser approach is designed to focus on the questions which need answering rather than to suggest that there is a unique set of policy answers which can be immediately and effectively applied. It is appropriate for use when there is no agreement about the real issues which are critical in a particular area of concern. Its use could therefore be effective today across a broad range of concerns.

A problem/possibility focuser gives a picture of the status of the debate on the subject under consideration on a continuing basis. Those engaged in producing it recognize that they will necessarily disagree: they try to find what can be understood and agreed which will clarify the nature of the real issues involved. Instead of looking for a technological fix, those involved in this approach accept the need for continued "messiness" in the culture.

The problem/possibility focuser approach can be applied to any geographical area and to any subject of real concern. For example, one can think about problem/possibility focusers on the water problem in Tucson, the educational issues in the central areas of Detroit, the nuclear power issues in the United States, and the global food problem. Problem/possibility focusers are also suitable for use within any institution: a business could use the technique to determine whether it should enter a new activity; a church could use it to discover what its attitude should be to poverty; an educational institution could use it to determine how to deal with the possibility of declining enrollments.

The existing conception of the problem/possibility focuser, which is, of course, still evolving, has four parts:

queries
and
comments

1. The first section describes the agreements which exist around a particular issue, especially the factors which cause people to accept that this is an issue which deserves continuing attention. Taking examples from the field of food one would list, among other issues: the maldistribution of worldwide food resources, the growing evidence of climatic shift, the existence of chronic malnutrition and some starvation, and the loss of arable land to bad farming practices and to building.

2. The second section describes the disagreements which exist around a particular issue, the reasons for the disagreements as best they can be determined, and the type of knowledge which would need to be developed if agreements were to be reached. Again in the field of food one might list among other areas:

   a. the degree to which the climate is actually shifting—a technical issue.
   b. fundamental disagreements about the impacts of land reform—a values issue and a disagreement about human behavior patterns.
   c. the potentials of controlled agriculture—a technical issue.
   d. the viability of triage and lifeboat-ethic strategies—a value and human behavior question.
   e. the impacts of the energy question—affected by facts, technological and human behavior questions.
   f. the growing understanding of the ecological impacts of fertilizer- and pesticide-intensive farming—a technical and value issue.

101

(Obviously the distinctions between facts, human behavior, technical and values issues are to some extent arbitrary: for example, if any issue is pushed far enough it becomes a values issue, for any accepted behavior is always based on cultural norms.)

3. The third section sets out the scenario implications of the various models being proposed and suggests the policy measures which would be needed depending on the various views. The different scenarios can then be challenged by those who disagree with them. Thus, to continue with the global food problem, there are some people who would argue that we need to take immediate large-scale measures to avoid worldwide famine and others who would argue that existing patterns of agriculture will make it possible to improve worldwide nutrition without "heroic" measures. There are some people who argue that our only hope is to abandon large parts of the worldwide population to starvation and others who claim that such a stance is both immoral and ineffective.

4. The fourth section would state the resources available for further understanding. The most important of these resources would be the people and groups who are working on various parts of the food issue—and related subjects. In addition, print, video, audio, and computer-based information would be included.

B. "Translation" of Problem/Possibility Focusers

As the previous section has shown, the idea behind a problem/possibility focuser is to create a document which reflects the current state of the debate on any particular topic. As such, it would be different from the present situation in which there is a continuing struggle between the proponents of different policy options.

An important benefit of the problem/possibility focuser technique is that it is ideally suited to take advantage of the potentials of the new electronic technologies. As we shall see later, it will be possible for the problem/possibility focuser to be updated rapidly as new information becomes available. This type of document will therefore tend to limit the problems which exist with present publishing techniques that result in severely out-of-date information.

However, the problem/possibility focuser would have only a limited effect if we did not deal with the different ways in which people learn. We need to begin, as a society, to make provision for "translation" to different types of media; this is required because the initial statement on a problem/possibility focuser will be made at a level which will not be easy for the general public to understand. We must therefore take steps to ensure that the knowledge we gain is made available to all levels of understanding from kindergarten upwards and also learn to use the various media in ways which are effective.

Moving to achieve this goal will be far more difficult than we presently understand. During the industrial era we believed that people received the message that was sent to them; that there was a tidy correlation between the teachings we aimed to make available and the information that people received. We now know that people's receipt of messages is mediated by an immensely complex screening process of the sense organs and the brain. We still understand far too little of the implications of this reality.

Some pioneering work has been done, of course. For example, Piaget has shown that there are some apparent patterns in terms of the ages at which children can learn certain skills and ideas. Some work has been done on sensory inputs. But in general we still pay very little attention to knowledge regarding the process of translation from the sent message to the received message.

C. Uses of Problem/Possibility Focusers

If an innovation is to have a chance of being significant, it should be demonstrated that there is a felt need for it. I do not think that it is difficult to meet this criterion in this case. The frustration with existing methods of structuring knowledge, the extraordinary difficulty in conducting research, and the grotesque overload of published material all point to the necessity of fundamental change in knowledge patterns.

Such a blanket statement may, however, be inadequate to convince people of the validity of the proposed approach. It may therefore be worthwhile to point out some of the ways in which information structured along these lines could be useful to public decision makers, private decision makers, educators, and the media.

I have already pointed out that the public decision maker is so overwhelmed by the noise of special pleading which exists around all important policy issues that he is often prevented from gaining any grasp of the really key possibilities and problems in any area. Assumptions and values are hidden by a frantic lobbying effort to achieve the goals which have been set by each group. I have discovered in personal conversations the interest legislators would have in

queries
and
comments

103

new forms of knowledge structuring which would provide some handles for decision making.

The private decision maker is equally in need of good information to determine the directions in which he should turn his attention. The manufacturer who continued to turn out buggy whips long after they were in a declining market is an example of a failure to reconceptualize the market in which one is active: if the buggy whip manufacturer had thought of himself in terms of being in the transportation industry he might well have survived. My discussions with corporate planners have shown me how difficult it is to get top management to take a look at new societal directions; problem/possibility focusers could play a role here.

One of the greatest gains would, of course, occur in education. At the present time most of the material which is available—whether in print, audio, or video form—is at best obsolescent and is quite often obsolete. This is inevitable given present patterns of publication. A computer-based problem/possibility focuser can, as has already been stated, be kept up to date on a continuing basis. In addition, an individual would no longer need to read or see several different presentations in order to get a perception of the extent and significance of the existing difference in views—the necessary information is all contained within a single document. Indeed, it seems reasonable to see the problem/possibility focuser as the base for the communications-era encyclopedia.

Finally, this problem/possibility focuser approach would necessarily have an extraordinary impact on the media and methods of reporting. The media are presently trapped by the need to report major stories in a fragmentary way. Each day they interview somebody who has a different slant on the story, and they dutifully report what they have learned to their public. Unfortunately, the overall impact of this style of reporting on the reader or viewer is to leave him or her increasingly baffled.

Wholistic, large-scale stories are outside the capacity of most of the media. Even when "in-depth" reporting is attempted it is within an objective frame. The viewer is told that he is only seeing "factual material." However, there is nearly always an implied or expressed conclusion—a slant—with which the public is expected to agree.

The problem/possibility focuser could alter this situation. It could provide people with an overall perception of the real differences that exist, the reasons *why* people disagree, and could also suggest the tools people could use to be involved in thinking about their own futures.

Obviously, these patterns of uses would change the socioeconomic and political system of the country. Problem/possibility focusers would enable people to have a better perception of the real issues which face us. We pay lip service to a well-informed democracy. Whether we are able and willing to take steps to create such a well-informed democracy is the issue which lies behind the problem/possibility focuser model and will determine the success of this mode.

queries
and
comments

D. Necessary Personal Skills

There are, of course, many possible objections to the problem/possibility focuser model. The primary question which nearly always emerges, however, is "Where are you going to find the people who are willing and able to work with knowledge systems in the way you describe? Obviously, everybody will try to distort the picture to ensure that they gain the maximum advantage."

I find this reaction fascinating. Any response to it must have several parts. First, I deny that I expect to set up a perfect system in which we shall know all that we need to know about any subject. I am not arguing that the result of a problem/possibility focuser system will be a pattern of knowledge which will answer every question we need to ask: rather I am stating that it should be within our competence to define the relevant questions that we need to be considering at this time when humanity is controlling the evolution of the earth.

Second, within this context, I state that we (all those involved) will choose the best people we can find for the initial work on any problem/possibility focuser. Obviously, the initial group will not be the final group: people will move in and out. There is no need to worry excessively about people staying when they cannot contribute because these groups will be made up of competent people—people who always have more to do than they can manage and who are delighted to give up any activity when their help is not needed to make an effort successful.

Third, these groups will contain people who have changed their perception of their self-interest. The group will consist of people who have recognized that their own development, the long-run success of the individuals and the institutions with which they are associated, and, indeed, the survival of the human race depend on fundamental changes in values and patterns toward more responsible behavior. Given this reality, it is not surprising that the people involved in the creation of problem/possibility focusers are prepared to try to understand the real issues rather than to set forth their narrowest self-interest.

Nevertheless, we must always remember that any movement toward a problem/possibility focuser format not only involves a shift in ways of structuring knowledge, it also requires fundamental changes in patterns of behavior. The shift from the industrial era to the communications era will demand alterations in perceptions and action patterns which are at least as far reaching as those which took place during the shift from the agricultural era to the industrial era. Thus, we are necessarily considering different skills than those which were taught by industrial-era societies—not merely an extension or addition to those which are already known.

E. Computer Implications

IBM has taken out double-spread ads in a number of magazines announcing that we are entering the information era. I find this significant at two levels:

1. It has long been a commonplace that the bulk of the income of the rich countries is generated through the information sector of the society. For IBM to make a fuss about this point at this late date shows that they believe this will be an effective sales point now.
2. More importantly, IBM is still clearly working out of industrial-era models and assuming that there are "facts" and "data" to be communicated efficiently and thus overlooking the need for interactive communication. As one looks at IBM, one is not surprised that they are caught in this pattern—indeed, my experience with other computer companies shows the same difficulties—but this does suggest that the computer experts will not be the ones who understand or bring into existence the true implications of the technologies they have invented.

In effect, we are still treating the computer as if it simply permits us to do the things we wanted to do in the industrial era better and faster. We are not recognizing that computers are forcing us into recognizing new authority patterns: computer-based knowledge systems are making it impossible for decisions to be imposed on the basis of power rather than knowledge. It is therefore somewhat amazing that many people concerned about social reform and change see the computer as a block to achieving a more democratic society rather than as the prime route toward it.

This does not mean that the required transition will be easy, but it does mean that if we come to accept the logic of the communications era—rather than the industrial era—we shall find that our society will be forced into a democratic mode. The problem/possibility focuser will be both chicken and egg in this process: helping people to see the possibilities and at the same time providing the structure for an alternative form of society.

Indeed, I have suggested that the problem/possibility focuser will be the basis for a new form of encyclopedia; using the word encyclopedia in its basic meaning—a way of organizing knowledge. In a sense each society and culture has to find a way of organizing knowledge which fits its conditions. I am suggesting that the problem/possibility focuser is the type of format which will be needed for an on-line, real-time system.

The development of a problem/possibility focuser model is urgent because of the inevitable speed of introduction of the new technologies: the nation will be wired by 1984. Very few people seem to be aware of the realities or the implications of this situation, and fundamental thinking is very sparse.

F. Methods of Drafting

The suggestion which follows is an idealized statement of the way in which early problem/possibility focusers can be drafted; the patterns and norms will necessarily change substantially as networks are established and the efforts are more fully computer based. It is assumed that a significant amount of face-to-face contact will be necessary for early problem/possibility focusers.

Step one

Choose a community where people are committed to improving the quality of life/patterns of behavior. This can be geographical, institutional—a community of interest or a group of people concerned about a shared problem or possibility.

It is essential, however, that there be a real shared set of concerns and understandings within the community—a sense of mutuality. This is often described today as the sharing of a *situational* communication style. The existence of this situational provides the potential energy for meaningful activities.

Step two

Choose ten to fifteen people from the community who are personally and heavily committed to improving the quality of life/patterns of behavior. Those chosen should represent the full range of responsible, informed, open opinion within the community.

This choice process is, of course, critical. If the panel is too narrow, there will be little prospect of a useful interchange of views,

queries
and
comments

If it includes people who are wed to an ideological viewpoint, the group will not change whatever is written.

Step three

Ask each person to provide answers to two questions, limiting the statements to 125 words.

1. What do you believe is the most vital step to improve the quality of life/patterns of behavior in the community? While each person should be free to choose any goal he or she wishes, emphasis would be placed on practical, workable steps.
2. What part of the accepted conventional wisdom in the community is the greatest block to effective decision making?

Step four

These statements would then be compiled; answers would be consolidated if they covered similar ground. Each of those involved would then be asked to react to this material in the following way:

For statement one.

A. On a scale of one to five, state how desirable you believe the suggested goal for the community would be.

B. On a scale of one to five, state how feasible you believe the chosen goal for the community is.

C. Write up to one hundred words in explanation of your responses.

For statement two.

A. On a scale of one to five, do you agree that people in the community have the view which is described in the response?

B. On a scale of one to five, assuming that the statement is correct (whether you agree with it or not) do you believe that such a view would get in the way of good decision making?

C. Write up to one hundred words in explanation of your response.

At the end of this round, there will be a sense of those issues on which there is consensus and those on which there is not and also some documentation, through the responses, as to the reasons.

Step five

Compile the material and circulate it. Provide the opportunity for each person to rethink his/her stance in the light of the comments which have been made.

queries
and
comments

There should be no pressure toward consensus at this stage. It will be as important to discover those areas in which there are real divergencies of opinion in the community as to show that there are some differences which are believed to be widespread but which are actually unimportant or nonexistent.

Step six

Publish the results using the available media, whether print, radio, TV, computers, etc.

There should be the opportunity for maximum feedback. For example, if the local newspaper can be interested then it would be ideal for the general public to have the same opportunity to respond to the original material and the feedback from the panel. Other media will provide other types of opportunities.

Step seven

Use this material as the basis for a meeting or meetings to begin to develop agreements about the most urgent steps which can be taken.

Step eight

Choose from those who have been identified during this overall process as showing commitment, a number of people who represent the various views about the issue under consideration and who are willing to work within the problem/possibility focuser format. It is suggested that the number should fall between eight and twelve in order to meet what we know about small group interactions. As already stated the group will not be "ideal," and we may well expect to see movement in and out of it. "Expertise" is not a condition for membership in the group but passionate interest and willingness to learn is.

Step nine

Bring this group and staff together for a three-day session. While work would certainly be done at this time to try to begin the process of understanding the patterns of agreement and disagreement, a great deal of the time would be taken up in getting to know members and establishing a situational for the group. Thus, play and games would be part of the first meeting; those people who did not recognize the need for good personal relationships in work of this sort would not be able to achieve a successful role in this overall effort.

The staff could be hired as full-time personnel if financial support was available in relative abundance. Another possibility could be to work with a professor and graduate students who would be excited by the possibility of working with first-class people in the field.

queries
and
comments

One possible approach for the work portion of this first meeting would be to ask each person to make one statement that she or he thought would be acceptable for the whole group. This could lead to one of two results: either there would be people present who would disagree, thus beginning to define the area of controversy, or there would be genuine agreement and this would form part of the agreement section of the document. Another critical goal for the meeting would be to define areas in which staff could do research and think.

Step ten

If at all possible, staff and participants would be linked at all times through a computer-based telecommunications system. The contact which would thus be possible would increase both the work and the relationship potential of the group. However, the success of early problem/possibility focuser creation does not depend on the availability of teleconferencing.

Step eleven

After a period of time for reflection—say two to three months —the group would come back together again. The purpose of this second meeting would be to create the first draft of a problem/possibility focuser which people would be prepared to have commented upon and criticized. If this goal could not be met at the second meeting, it would have to be put off till the third, but I believe that it would be both important and possible to begin to see some written results after the second meeting.

Step twelve

Comments, ideas, and responses would be solicited from those most competent in the field; circulation would be kept relatively limited during this period to avoid overloading all those involved. It should be expected that people will have difficulty understanding the difference between the problem/possibility focuser and existing methods of knowledge structuring; efforts would have to be made to ensure that this understanding was achieved, for otherwise many of the comments would be useless. During this period, efforts would also be made to contact media, publishers, and "translators." Further meetings of the group would take place.

Step thirteen

Feedback would continue. Plans would be laid for initial publication and translation.

Step fourteen

The problem/possibility focuser would be approved for widespread publication. The feedback and revision process would, of course, continue as long as the issue was important.

Your Involvement

Books alone are not effective methods of bringing about change. There are profound reasons for this reality.

Alterations in personal perception—the key to changed action patterns—take place at the intersection of three factors:
—First, a reconsideration of the forces which have caused one's present pattern of behavior, desires, and beliefs so that it can then be changed if desirable. Until we are committed to such a reconsideration, we shall continue to be driven by the forces we have inherited and developed through our unique genetic and experiential pattern.
—Second, a reconceptualization of the future we desire. This can alter either the goals we want or the means we believe will be effective for reaching them. It will recognize, however, that the future is created on the basis of self-fulfilling and self-denying prophecies and that what we do will alter inevitably, in small or large ways, the situation in which we live, the experience of those around us, and just possibly the total world of which we are a part.
—Third, through action which begins change processes. As we learn from our own experience, we will bring about a slow evolution of our behavior toward more healthy patterns.

Effective change therefore normally requires the availability of small-scale human interactive patterns where people work on a caring, committed level to help each other learn to act in new ways. Many programs of this type have developed across the United States in the last decade: the community/neighborhood movement is indeed one of the liveliest forces that exists at the present time.

There are also, of course, other communities that are committed to change that do not work on a face-to-face basis. Professional and intellectual groups may work over long distances through various forms of network and linking systems. The increasing pervasiveness of various forms of telecommunications, including computer-based teleconferencing, makes these approaches ever more effective.

The problem is, of course, that we are all "booby trapped" by our past understandings and least likely to be helpful when we are most certain of our ground. For example, we know in theory that the creation of synergetic solutions to problems depends on cooperative behavior. But the neighborhood and community movement often still works with the models developed by Saul Alinsky who essentially saw success as "beating" the establishment rather than helping both the establishment and the community group perceive the need for new goals. Still, other movements encourage people to turn inwards. These fail to examine and work to change the socioeconomic systems which are increasingly hostile to human and humane patterns of behavior.

There are many apparent conflicts which could be resolved if we would commit ourselves to an overall pattern of rethinking outside the straight jacket of conventional understandings. Many communities are frustrated, for example, by the incredible waste of energy which exists when teen-agers are idle—not to speak of the inevitable vandalism, crime, and the potential for riots. Instead of searching for new, creative, community-based styles of work which would also develop community pride, there is still almost general acceptance of the belief that sufficient industrial-style jobs can and will be generated and that each geographical area should strive to bring jobs into it even at high environmental and financial costs.

If we are to achieve urgently necessary changes, we must somehow mesh the raw energy of the various movements which exist to correct injustices with information about desirable and feasible long-run directions. This is the way in which true differences in dynamics could be developed.

What is the greatest block to the successful development of such a pattern? I suspect that it is to a large extent the conviction of those who have been the gatekeepers of knowledge in the past that the general public is not interested and not intelligent. It is my personal conviction that current difficulties do not result from lack of interest or intelligence but from the determination of all too many intellectuals that people should learn intellectually rather than in terms of the felt needs of the individual, the group, and the community.

The result of this viewpoint has been the opening of an enormous chasm between what is taught in schools, colleges, and universities and what is learned through the realities of the world. One of the rare exceptions is the agricultural extension service which tries to inform farmers' and citizens' direct and immediate needs. Another great potential, which has so far been largely vitiated, is the community college movement.

Our real need today is to provide new patterns of information to meet felt needs. To achieve such a goal, we need to create new channels of communication. There are meaningful roles in this overall task for those who are concerned about the direction of our society and have the energy to change it.

You can be involved if you want to be. Today's problem is not primarily a lack of information or skills: it is a shortage of willpower and courage. If we fail to create new conditions, it will be because we were not *willing* to act rather than because we did not know how to be effective.

At the present time, a number of individuals and organizations are acting to make the new era we are entering visible and viable. If their activities are successful, one of the news stories of the year 1984 might be:

ORWELL INSTITUTE CREATED

The Orwell Institute was created today by various groups across the United States which have been cooperating with increasing closeness over the last few years. They have been acting together to enable people to understand the fundamental revolutions in weaponry that have made war obsolete, the revolution in production and management based on the computer, and the revolution in human rights which has increased the skills of young people and their demands for creative opportunities.

Jane Smith, a spokesperson for the group, stated that the new organization was being called the Orwell Foundation because it was being created in 1984. It therefore seemed highly appropriate to honor the role which had been played by George Orwell through his book *1984* in alerting us to the dangers of this period of history.

The organizations involved all agree that we are engaged in a fundamental transformation from the industrial era to the communications era which is forcing major shifts in life style and life cycle. "This overall perception has developed rapidly during the eighties," Smith said. "The extraordinary challenges of the rapid transition from one set of conditions to another is more and more widely recognized," she added.

The Orwell Institute will support, develop, and enlarge patterns of activity which have been developing through the previously informal collaboration among the involved groups. Among the most critical patterns will be:

—provision of information about the processes of change in America and throughout the world as a result of the work of the communications store.

—development of vibrant, local networking groups which ensure that effective cross-contacts are made between concerned, action-oriented citizens so that synergies can be achieved.

—availability of national, and increasingly transnational, linkage patterns so that if a required contact is not available within a local community or region, the relevant person can be discovered elsewhere.

—opportunities for face-to-face contact between those most heavily involved in effective transformational activities who cannot find a "critical mass" within their own geographical area.

AVOIDING 1984

queries
and
comments

These activities, with the exception of the fourth, are already being carried out by each organization. Both fund-raising needs and the necessity to demonstrate national viability have led to the decision to create a national foundation at this time. Each separate organization will, however, retain full autonomy.

The cooperating nonprofit groups are based in communities which permit effective regionalization: there are local contacts in most cities and towns and some villages.

Would you like to be part of the process which might make this news story a self-fulfilling prophecy? If you would, then write, enclosing a stamped, addressed envelope, to Box 2240, Wickenburg, Arizona 85385. If you do write, and if all goes well (which it won't, of course) between the date the drafting of this book is completed and the date of its appearance, we should be able to provide information on:

—effective transformational programs in several communities.
—statewide or regionwide programs to enable citizens to get involved in creating their own future.
—a "communications store" aiming to select the best information on the theoretical and practical implications of the transformation.
—names of contacts in a number of cities who have committed themselves to introducing people to transformational ideas.
—opportunities to develop your understanding and commitment to as broad and as deep a level as you may wish.

In order to avoid misunderstandings let me stress that these systems will not help you significantly if your goal is to be a passive recipient of ideas. *You must want to act on the basis of a growing understanding.* Second, there will be a modest charge for involvement and, like everybody else, we'll always be in need of more funds than we have.

On the other hand, I believe that this effort can make a difference. I look forward to hearing from those of you who share this view.